Reading Spinoza in the Anthropocene

Spinoza Studies
Series editor: Filippo Del Lucchese, Alma Mater Studiorum – Università di Bologna

Seminal works devoted to Spinoza that challenge mainstream scholarship
This series aims to broaden the understanding of Spinoza in the Anglophone world by making some of the most important work by continental scholars available in English translation for the first time. Some of Spinoza's most important themes – that right is coextensive with power, that every political order is based on the power of the multitude, the critique of superstition and the rejection of the idea of providence – are explored by these philosophers in detail and in ways that will open up new possibilities for reading and interpreting Spinoza.

Editorial Advisory board
Saverio Ansaldi, Etienne Balibar, Chiara Bottici, Laurent Bove, Mariana de Gainza, Moira Gatens, Thomas Hippler, Susan James, Chantal Jaquet, Mogens Laerke, Beth Lord, Pierre Macherey, Nicola Marcucci, Alexandre Matheron (1926–2020), Dave Mesing, Warren Montag, Pierre-François Moreau, Vittorio Morfino, Antonio Negri, Susan Ruddick, Martin Saar, Pascal Sévérac, Hasana Sharp, Diego Tatián, Francesco Toto, Dimitris Vardoulakis, Lorenzo Vinciguerra, Stefano Visentin, Manfred Walther, Caroline Williams.

Books available
Affects, Actions and Passions in Spinoza: The Unity of Body and Mind, Chantal Jaquet, translated by Tatiana Reznichenko
The Spinoza–Machiavelli Encounter: Time and Occasion, Vittorio Morfino, translated by Dave Mesing
Politics, Ontology and Knowledge in Spinoza, Alexandre Matheron, translated and edited by Filippo Del Lucchese, David Maruzzella and Gil Morejón
Spinoza, the Epicurean: Authority and Utility in Materialism, Dimitris Vardoulakis
Experience and Eternity in Spinoza, Pierre-François Moreau, edited and translated by Robert Boncardo
Spinoza and the Politics of Freedom, Dan Taylor
Spinoza's Political Philosophy: The Factory of Imperium, Riccardo Caporali, translated by Fabio Gironi
Spinoza's Paradoxical Conservatism, François Zourabichvili, translated by Gil Morejón
Marx with Spinoza: Production, Alienation, History, Franck Fischbach, translated by Jason Read
Time, Duration and Eternity in Spinoza, Chantal Jaquet, translated by Eric Aldieri
Affirmation and Resistance in Spinoza: The Strategy of the Conatus, Laurent Bove, translated and edited by Émilie Filion-Donato and Hasana Sharp
Reading Spinoza in the Anthropocene, Genevieve Lloyd

Forthcoming
Spinoza and Contemporary Biology: Lectures on the Philosophy of Biology and Cognitivism, Henri Atlan, translated by Inja Stracenski and Robert Boncardo
Spinoza's Critique of Hobbes: Law, Power and Freedom, Christian Lazzeri, translated by Nils F. Schott
Spinoza and the Sign: The Logic of Imagination, Lorenzo Vinciguerra, translated by Alexander Reynolds
New Perspectives on Spinoza's Theologico-Political Treatise: Politics, Power and the Imagination, edited by Dan Taylor and Marie Wuth
Passions and Politics in Spinoza, Diego Tatián, translated by Nicolas Allen
Democratic Thought from Machiavelli to Spinoza, Sonja Lavaert, translated by Albert Gootjes

Visit our website at www.edinburghuniversitypress.com/series/SPIN

Reading Spinoza in the Anthropocene

Genevieve Lloyd

EDINBURGH
University Press

Edinburgh University Press is one of the leading university presses in the UK. We publish academic books and journals in our selected subject areas across the humanities and social sciences, combining cutting-edge scholarship with high editorial and production values to produce academic works of lasting importance. For more information visit our website: edinburghuniversitypress.com

© Genevieve Lloyd, 2024, 2025

Edinburgh University Press Ltd
13 Infirmary Street
Edinburgh EH1 1LT

First published in hardback by Edinburgh University Press 2024

Typeset in 10.5/13 Goudy Old Style
by Cheshire Typesetting Ltd, Cuddington, Cheshire

A CIP record for this book is available from the British Library

ISBN 978 1 3995 3336 2 (hardback)
ISBN 978 1 3995 3337 9 (paperback)
ISBN 978 1 3995 3338 6 (webready PDF)
ISBN 978 1 3995 3339 3 (epub)

The right of Genevieve Lloyd to be identified as the author of this work has been asserted in accordance with the Copyright, Designs and Patents Act 1988, and the Copyright and Related Rights Regulations 2003 (SI No. 2498).

Contents

Acknowledgements	vi
Spinoza Texts and Abbreviations	vii
Introduction: Spinoza in a Contemporary Context	1
1. 'God' and 'Nature'	10
2. Embodied Knowing	31
3. The Whole Mind	58
4. The Power of the Human Mind	84
5. Beyond Reason	116
6. Alternative Interpretations	133
7. Rethinking the Present	147
8. Imagining the Future	168
Conclusion: 'Descartes' and 'Spinoza'	182
Bibliography	187
Index	194

Acknowledgements

Earlier versions of some sections of my discussion of Spinoza's version of reason were published as an essay 'Reconsidering Spinoza's "Rationalism"' – along with my responses to commentators – in the *Australasian Philosophical Review*, vol. 4, issue no. 3, 2020. I am grateful to the editors, and to the curator of the issue, Joanne Faulkner, for the opportunity to participate in that project, and for helpful advice and suggestions during the process. I wish also to express my appreciation to the commentators for their thoughtful critiques of the original essay: Sandra Field, Moira Gatens, Steph Marston, Anne Newstead, Knox Peden, Michael Rosenthal and Walter Veit.

My understanding of Spinoza's philosophy has been greatly enriched over several years by exchange of ideas with Australian scholars and students of Spinoza. In relation to the thinking that shaped this book, I am grateful especially for the stimulus of engagement with Aurelia Armstrong, Robert Boncardo, Justin Clemens, Moira Gatens, Joe Hughes, Janice Richardson, Jon Rubin, Inja Stracenski, Anthony Uhlmann and Dimitris Vardoulakis.

I wish also to express my gratitude for constructive feedback from the Publisher for Philosophy at University of Edinburgh Press, Carol Macdonald; the Spinoza Studies Series Editor, Filippo Del Lucchese; and two anonymous manuscript reviewers.

Spinoza Texts and Abbreviations

The Ethics [1677], in Curley, Edwin, ed. and trans., *The Collected Works of Spinoza*, Vol. I (Princeton: Princeton University Press, 1985), pp. 408–617.

Theological-Political Treatise [1670], in Curley, Edwin, ed. and trans. *The Collected Works of Spinoza*, Vol. II (Princeton: Princeton University Press, 2016), pp. 65–354.

Political Treatise [1677], in Curley, Edwin, ed. and trans., *The Collected Works of Spinoza*, Vol. II (Princeton: Princeton University Press, 2016), pp. 503–604.

The five Parts of the *Ethics* are identified as *Ethics I*, *Ethics II*, *Ethics III*, *Ethics IV* and *Ethics V*.

References to the text of the *Ethics* are made in accordance with the following abbreviations:

A	Axiom
Cor.	Corollary
D	Definition
Dem.	Demonstration
E	the *Ethics*
Exp.	Explanation
L	Lemma
P	Proposition
Schol.	Scholium
Sec.	Section

Introduction: Spinoza in a Contemporary Context

Not many disagreements among philosophers break through the nuances or niceties of academic exchange to enter contested arenas of public discourse. On occasion, though, an episode from the history of philosophical thought will take on a new significance in relation to some pressing issue of human well-being which seems to challenge prevailing ways of thinking. In present times, how to conceptualise human presence in the natural world has become such an issue. The need to rethink humanity's place in Nature has become a prevalent theme in contemporary discussion of the challenges of climate change.

In that context, there is a cluster of mantras that are constantly reiterated in public discourse, yet seldom directly addressed: that human beings must learn to see themselves as part of Nature; that they should cease to regard themselves as superior, or as rightfully dominant, in relation to the non-human; that they should follow Nature, rather than trying to subdue or control it; that their own survival and thriving is interconnected with that of the whole of Nature.

What exactly might it be for a human mind to seriously engage with the notion that it is itself but part of the natural world, with no privileged position within it? How might that affect collective understanding of human presence on a changing planet? What readily evades philosophical scrutiny here is that, despite common repudiation of 'Cartesian dualism', climate change discourse can be pervaded by an implicit assumption that human thought is itself somehow positioned outside Nature.

Human bodies may be readily recognised as part of the natural world. Yet human minds continue to imagine themselves in ways that are in tension with that recognition. There is a deep, and largely unnoticed, conceptual challenge in impasses in current discussion of climate change. Often what is at play is not so much reaching factual agreement, as knowing how to appropriately imagine the relations between thought and Nature.

Spinoza and Descartes

In a famous seventeenth-century philosophical exchange, Spinoza suggested that adherence to Descartes's treatment of the nature and status of human knowing was not just a theoretical error, but a deep failure of imagination. He regarded the Cartesian way of imagining certainty as itself a misconstrual of what it is to be a human thinker. As Spinoza saw it, Descartes was in error about the very nature of error: his mistake rested on a flawed imagining of a human mind's own status in relation to non-human parts of the world.

The details of Spinoza's critique of the Cartesian model of knowledge are elaborated in Part II of his most famous work, the *Ethics*. The ground for exposing what he saw as erroneous in that model is prepared in Part I of the work – in the definitions of substance, attributes and modes. The consequences of the mistaken Cartesian model for understanding the power of human reason are explored in Parts III and IV of the *Ethics*. Finally, in Part V, Spinoza sketches what he sees as the upshot for human well-being of his own alternative way of construing human thought.

The *Ethics* tracks the journey of a mind letting go of deep misapprehensions of its own nature, and of its relations with the whole of Nature – of its place within the totality of things. The work is not just a structure of theoretical argumentation; it is an enactment of a mind's release from a misunderstanding of its own being.

On the reading I will offer, the *Ethics* does not merely argue for rejection of Descartes's theory of the nature of human knowing. It shows Spinoza repudiating, in his own philosophical practice, the treatment of reason as a higher, independently operating faculty, which rightly dominates or suppresses imagination and emotion. The work's structure unfolds as a realisation of the inter-relations and interactions of those different aspects of human thinking.

The Supremacy of Reason

A long history of philosophical views on reason plays out in tensions within Spinoza's writings. An even longer history of those views comes to the surface in the inchoate notions of reason that contemporary readers, consciously or unconsciously, bring to the texts. Some of those notions were formed within thought later than the times of Descartes and Spinoza – in philosophies of the eighteenth and nineteenth centuries, which were themselves influenced by limited understanding of Spinoza. Others have accrued from twentieth-century philosophy, in which the reading of Spinoza has often been shaped by inflexible categories of 'rationalism' and 'empiricism' which elide the rich nuances of his thought.

Of the many themes around the concept of reason that Western philosophy has helped to articulate – and out of the many 'Spinozas' that its history has bequeathed to the world – the issue that most clearly bears on contemporary climate change issues is the contested notion of the supremacy of reason. It comes in two forms: the supremacy of human minds in relation to the rest of the world; and, within the human mind, the dominance of reason over other aspects of being human – sensory awareness, imagination, emotion.

In the thought of Romanticism, the inter-relation of those two spheres of supremacy was given clear – though not uncontroversial – formulation in terms of a distinction between 'Nature without' and 'Nature within' the human mind. It was in some ways a confusing contrast. Yet it captured a sense of connection between a mind's confrontation with the non-human parts of the world and awareness of its own internal division. Reason was presented as the mark of superiority and entitlement, both within the totality of being and within an individual mind.

Some elements from the Cartesian model of knowledge underlie contemporary notions of human supremacy over the rest of

Nature, along with exultation in the powers of reason inherited from later Romanticism. Hence, to read Spinoza attentively now can yield confrontation with assumptions about the relations between human and non-human which are at play in current debate on climate change.

Human and Non-human

The interdependence of human and non-human is not an insight that had to await either Spinoza or recent narratives of the Anthropocene. Rather than being a new development in human history, that interdependence is a precondition of human life itself. Yet the full realisation of the implications of interdependence has often been blocked by the ways in which it has been imagined.

Spatial imagery played a central role in the Cartesian way of construing relations between human and non-human, which Spinoza repudiated. Spinoza's critique emphasised the territorial associations which he thought shaped Descartes's understanding of human presence in the world: locating human beings in Nature as like a kingdom within a kingdom. It is not just a spatial metaphor, but a quasi-political one, evoking not just a territory but a sovereign domain – with laws unto itself, unaffected by the necessities that 'govern' the rest of Nature. Human free will is thereby figured as marking a border which demarcates not only human powers, but also human rights and privileges.

There are also temporal connotations in common ways of regarding human presence in the world. Human beings are construed as having emerged out of mere Nature into a superior condition. That notion became more clearly articulated in association with the impact of evolutionary theory, though it was already inchoately present in earlier talk of stages of human development. Those temporal associations of human presence facilitate thinking of the impact of human agency on the planet as a relatively recent development, rather than as a constant feature of the interrelations which have shaped both human and non-human.

Some of the tensions within contemporary climate change discourse, to be discussed in this book, arise from unresolved confusions about how those shifting relations between human and non-human are to be imagined. Language through which contemporary climate change concerns are expressed can itself perpetuate both spatial and temporal metaphors, which obfuscate the construal of interdependence, even while affirming it. Human beings are then readily seen as separated from an inert realm on which they exert a distinctive agency. Thus, even talk of 'the environment' can carry implicit reference to an assumed priority of human presence – like a spatial centre, around which the non-human falls into a subsidiary location.

A conceptual prioritising of what is human can be discerned also in the temporal connotations of more recent talk of the Anthropocene. In its most literal sense, the term gestures towards a tentative hypothesis of a new geological age, marked by changes in the structure of the Earth under human influence. In a broader application, it evokes a relatively recent period of human history, which has seen an acceleration of global warming under harmful impacts of human agency.

This book addresses a range of ways in which thought can be construed as 'human-centred'. Some of them are both harmless and unavoidable. Others are misleading and counterproductive, encouraging a view of human agency in itself as somehow deleterious for the rest of Nature. By offering a reading of Spinoza in the context of contemporary climate change discourse, the book aims to illuminate some of the tensions and confusions that arise within those debates.

Reading and Interpreting

Reading Spinoza now can offer a way into confused and contested issues that cluster around challenges to the supremacy of reason. In the following chapters, I will try to tease out how some understanding of his philosophy might enrich discussion of those issues. However, it must first be acknowledged that interpretation of Spinoza's version of reason is itself a strongly contested topic in contemporary textual commentary.

Extricating a philosophical disagreement from its historical context, in order to bring it to bear on contemporary issues, can be a challenging exercise. To ignore historical context can be to misinterpret the content of a text. Yet to leave that content embedded in its own intellectual and social context can be to impoverish it, to miss significant opportunities to illuminate the present.

The Cartesian model of human knowing, which Spinoza repudiated, lingers in contemporary ways of thinking of human and non-human. The familiarity of that model can mask its contingency. Assumptions, left unquestioned, can seem to represent an inevitable stage in human thought, rather than one among other intellectual paths that might have been followed. That can blind contemporary thinking to ways in which those contingent assumptions continue to shape, and to limit, collective imagining of human futures.

To offer a reading of a text in the history of philosophy is a different project from that of scholarly interpretation. Yet the two are interconnected, and in some ways inseparable. A reading is inherently selective in what it highlights – as indeed is any exercise in interpretation. No reading can cover all aspects of a text; and any interpretation is open to challenge on what it has left out of consideration. That may involve confrontation with uncomfortable quotations that have been overlooked. It may also involve reconsidering the significance of neglected aspects of the text, which might not have been given due salience.

The distinction between reading and interpretation does not align neatly with more familiar contrasts between past-centred and present-centred approaches to textual studies. Sensitive interpretation is attentive to historical context – both to the immediate context of the work itself, and to its intellectual background. Yet making that context prominent may also require being attuned to how it differs from contexts more familiar to present-day readers.

It may seem that a reading, in contrast to an interpretation, is more directly concerned with the present – with issues to which the text is deemed relevant. Yet, to avoid being anachronistic, a reading must involve a great deal more than mining a text for nuggets of insight that can be readily applied in a new context. It needs to be constrained by informed scholarship, offering a reasoned application – rather than a facile appropriation – to a new setting.

In practice, it may be largely a matter of emphasis that distinguishes a scholarly interpretation from a reading, informed by scholarship. To do either well demands a capacity to shift reflectively between an orientation towards the past and engagement with the present. Both approaches to a text require attention to envisaged readership. A scholarly interpretation, pitched to recognised experts on a particular historical period, will differ – in style and tone, as well as density – from a study directed to a more general audience. Yet here, too, the difference can be in practice one of degree.

Scholarly interpretations will be better if their imagined readership is not confined to those who know at least as much as the authors themselves. On the other hand, a self-consciously 'popular' account of past philosophy can lapse, all too easily, into tedious reconstruction. A preoccupation with accessibility can, by leaving out what is deemed too obscure or too difficult, deaden the original vitality – the movement of thought within the text.

My intention is to offer a reading of Spinoza in the context of a human world increasingly perplexed and troubled by the manifestations of planetary change. My central concern will be to articulate and critique a common way of imagining the relations between 'human' and 'non-human' within the totality of being. In the course of doing that, I hope also to challenge a prevailing conception of the character of Spinoza's philosophy.

Spinoza and 'Rationalism'

A common way of reading the *Ethics* reflects, and reinforces, a way of locating the figure of Spinoza in the context of more recent philosophy. He is often presented through a persona of arch 'rationalist' – strongly committed to the superiority and dominance of reason over supposedly lesser human capacities of sensory experience, imagination and emotion.

There is a kernel of truth in the representation of Spinoza's philosophy as epitomising the philosophical theory of knowledge that has come to be known as 'rationalism'. In his treatment of knowledge in *Ethics II*, he does treat reason as a higher form of knowledge than the more immediate deliverances of sensation, memory or imagination. He does present reason as the source of adequate knowledge of the natures of things, and hence as a way of thinking more attuned to rigorous intellectual inquiry.

It is also true that, later in the *Ethics*, Spinoza associates the exercise of reason with an idealised intellectual character. For him, a human life that cultivates reason is a free life, in which the destructive effects of debilitating passions can be overcome. Yet reason is not for Spinoza the highest kind of human knowledge; that place is reserved for what he calls 'intuitive knowledge'. While not abandoning reason, that higher form of understanding brings to bear on its exercise a transformed kind of imagination.

The reading I will offer emphasises aspects of the *Ethics* that pull against a familiar construction of Spinoza as epitomising what later came to be known as 'rationalism'. My reading presents him as offering a more nuanced version of human reason, stressing its integration with imagination and emotion, rather than dominance over them. That reading of Spinoza will, I hope, help clarify what is at issue in some familiar but contentious contemporary attitudes, which connect reason's assumed supremacy within a human mind with humanity's supposed supremacy within Nature.

To expose a flaw in the way human thought is construed is a different exercise from offering a viable alternative model. Spinoza attempts to do both. It may well be that his exposure of Descartes's flawed model of human knowing will prove, for contemporary readers, more accessible and plausible than his own breathtaking alternative philosophical vision in its entirety.

Yet, at the very least, reading Spinoza now can yield insight into understanding how past thought has shaped ways in which human presence in the world is commonly imagined. My hope is that this may serve to open space for fruitful reconceptualising of the impacts of climate change. I hope also that, along the way, this exercise in reading, interpreting and attempting to apply Spinoza's philosophy will not only provide constructive provocation to those who have read him differently, but encourage others to read him for the first time.

Structure and Strategy

Reflecting its character as a reading, this book mirrors in its structure that of the *Ethics*. Thus, the first five chapters track the sequence of the five parts of the *Ethics*, which Spinoza enumerates as: I. Of God; II. Of the Nature and Origin of the Mind; III. Of the Origin and Nature of the Affects; IV. Of Human Bondage, or of the Powers of the Affects; V. Of the Power of the Intellect or of Human Freedom.

Where relevant, I make diversions into Spinoza's political writings. However, the central thread in the argumentative strategy of these chapters is Spinoza's repudiation of Descartes's model of human knowing. Along the way, there are also comparisons with other figures in the history of Western philosophy, which help clarify just how Spinoza's philosophy can be brought to bear on contemporary climate change discussion.

Throughout Chapters 1–5, the argumentation moves between direct textual discussion and its application to climate change debate. What is offered is thus a reading of Spinoza in a contemporary context. Its juxtapositions of past and present aim to highlight affinities and dissonances between Spinoza's philosophy and some current ways of thinking, in order to prompt constructive rethinking.

Against that background, Chapter 6 stands back to consider alternative approaches to the *Ethics* that have been taken by other commentators – and some tensions within the text itself which might seem to call into question my attempted applications to the present. Chapters 7 and 8 then offer a summation of what has emerged towards reconceptualising climate change issues, in ways that may help move beyond some of the impasses of current debates.

The book concludes with some reflections on its methodology, centred on how constructs of 'Descartes' and 'Spinoza' figure in contemporary philosophical thought; on the distance of those figures from the historical Descartes and Spinoza; and on the positive role that contrasting those constructs may nonetheless play in applying the history of philosophy to contemporary issues.

1
'God' and 'Nature'

In the context of climate change, the idea of Nature is both familiar and elusive. Within it are accretions of past philosophical ideas and systems – often in tension with one another. Contemporary ways of thinking have been influenced, especially, by a residue from the ambiguities and ambivalences that developed around ideas of Nature in the philosophical thought and literary culture of Romanticism.

To read Spinoza now is to be immediately confronted with the strangeness of a philosophy which drew on elements from a wide range of earlier systems, yet made out of them something quite new. The novelty of his system's treatment of human thought within the totality of being influenced the spirit of Romanticism – though its implications may have been largely misconstrued in the process of its appropriation. In a contemporary context of life on a changing planet, the very strangeness of Spinoza's thought can open up possibilities for rethinking some crucial assumptions about human presence in Nature.

The Idea of Nature in Romanticism

Spinoza is now – to a large extent, unavoidably – understood through what Romanticism made of him. That construction of the figure of 'Spinoza' was mediated through, and coloured by, the construal of relations between reason and Nature in post-Kantian philosophy.

For thinkers associated with Romanticism, Nature was readily associated with the aesthetic pleasure that human beings take in the world which they inhabit. However, that aesthetic response was not confined to the appreciation of natural beauties. The Romantics' fascination with Nature was also imbued with a concept which was contrasted with the beautiful – the sublime.

The concept of the 'sublime', like that of Nature, had many sources in ancient thought. The distinctive eighteenth-century associations of the two concepts came largely through revival of a fragment of a work known as *On the Sublime*, dating probably from the first century CE, and attributed to Longinus. Edmund Burke – and, subsequently, Immanuel Kant – articulated this revised sense of 'the sublime' as a contrast term to 'the beautiful'. Burke's *Philosophical Enquiry into the Sublime and the Beautiful* was published in 1757; and Kant's early essay *Observations on the Feeling of the Beautiful and the Sublime*, in 1764. Kant later returned to the concept of the Sublime, developing it much more fully as a core theme in his *Critique of Judgement*, published in 1790.[1]

For later Romantic thought, one of the most important insights from Burke's *Enquiry* was that the exercise of human reason is largely bypassed by the feeling of the sublime. On his account, that feeling operates on the human mind independently of reason; it takes precedence over the effort to think rationally. Far from being produced by reasonings, he says, the feeling of the sublime anticipates them, hurrying thought on by an irresistible force. This feeling is an intensely emotional experience – a mixture of pain and pleasure, associated with power and with fear. Reverential awe is here mingled with turbulent astonishment. The feeling of the sublime is 'a sort of tranquillity, shadowed with horror'.[2]

For Burke, whereas reason has connotations of clear thinking and precision, the sublime abhors clarity – thriving instead on vagueness and confusion. Nor does it have any particular associations with strength of intellectual character. Burke distanced himself from praise of the sublime associated with the trait which

---

[1] I discuss eighteenth and nineteenth century developments in the concept of the sublime more fully in *Reclaiming Wonder: After the Sublime*; Lloyd 2018a: Chs 3 and 4.
[2] Burke 2015: Part I, Sec. III, p. 30.

Longinus had called 'greatness of soul'. Burke's sublime was nonetheless supposed to produce a sense of self-worth, a kind of 'glorifying' of self – a conviction of 'inward greatness'. He described it as producing 'a sort of swelling and triumph that is extremely grateful to the human mind'. Despite its associations with fear, human minds experiencing the sublime are supposed to find themselves exultant, rather than weakened.[3]

Kant, in his early essay on the topic, also emphasised the intensity of the feeling of the sublime. However, for him this feeling has greater internal complexity, and its relations with reason are more nuanced than in Burke's analysis. Although, in the case of what Kant calls 'the terrifying sublime', it can be associated with dread or melancholy, it can also – as the 'noble sublime' – take the form of quiet wonder.[4] So, even in this early version, Kant's feeling of the sublime is not polarised from calm, rational thinking.

In Kant's fuller development of the concept in the *Critique of Judgement*, the sublime comes into close connection with the mind's capacity for reason, thus entering into a new configuration of mental capacities. This later version of the sublime retains from Burke the connotations of vagueness – of formlessness or indeterminacy. However, that indeterminacy is now articulated in terms of what Kant calls an indeterminate concept of reason. Rather than simply bypassing rational thought, it is explicitly associated with a struggle between reason and imagination. Reason, regarded by Kant as the superior faculty, is elicited in the mind by the imagination's struggle to apprehend what lies ever beyond its capacities.

Burke had talked of the feeling of the sublime as a triumphant 'swelling' of the mind in realising its own powers. In Kant's mature version of the concept, that triumph is celebrated as a victory of reason. However, this noble outcome is not presented as a suppression of the turbulence of imagination or emotion. The mental turbulence is not left behind once reason has won the struggle. Rather, the end result is what Kant describes as a 'discordant accord' between rival faculties of the mind.

---

[3] Ibid. Part I, Sec. XVII, p. 43.
[4] Kant 1960: 47–8.

The crucial point here is that the Kantian sublime comes to be located, not primarily in objects of thought, but in thought itself. The sublime is now explicitly a cast of mind. 'True sublimity', Kant insists, 'must be sought only in the mind of the judging Subject, and not in the Object of nature that occasions this attitude by the estimate formed of it'.[5] It must in every case 'have reference to our *way of thinking*' (original emphasis). The sublime remains for Kant a feeling of great intensity and power. Yet it belongs with 'the intellectual side of our nature – with reason's supremacy over mere "sensibility"'.[6]

In the context of contemporary responses to climate change, what is important here is that, with this change, comes a significant shift in construing the human mind's relations with Nature. Kant says that the sublime resides, not only in reason's power over 'nature within', but also over 'nature without'.[7] It arises in the recognition of 'reason's extraordinary power of resistance over the apparent omnipresence of mere nature'. Notwithstanding the physical might and power of Nature, the mind comes to realise 'the appropriate sublimity of the sphere of its own being, even above nature'.[8]

This shift of emphasis to reason's power in relation to Nature is a notable development in the intellectual history of the relations between human and non-human. It also articulates a shift in the positioning of reason in relation to other human thought processes. The supremacy of reason over 'nature within' is here explicitly aligned with its supremacy over 'nature without'. That alignment lingers in contemporary discourse on the challenges of climate change.

Spinoza and Romanticism

The literary culture of Romanticism is associated with celebration of the wonders of the natural world; and with the cultivation of imagination and emotion, as distinct from the arid deliverances of

---

[5] Kant 1952: Part I, Book II, p. 104.
[6] Ibid. 127.
[7] Ibid. 114.
[8] Ibid. 111–12.

reason. If the tensions here are construed as a conflict, Romantic thinkers are on the side of imagination and emotion. Yet it is also possible to discern, in their interconnection of reason with the sublime, intimations of the ultimate supremacy of human reason over non-human Nature. Within the heritage of Romantic celebrations of 'nature without', lurks the notion that human relations with Nature are appropriately construed in terms of superiority and dominance.

The reception of Spinoza among thinkers associated with Romanticism was volatile. There were vexed debates about whether particular authors were influenced – or perhaps tainted – by his alleged pantheism. According to some, Spinoza treated God as disappearing into Nature. For others, on the contrary, Spinoza's philosophy seemed to contain too much God – a view famously held by the poet Novalis, who described him as a God-intoxicated man. It was an issue that helped shape discussion of a related dilemma in the repercussions of post-Kantian idealism: did the knowing human mind disappear into Nature? Or was it, rather, that the world disappeared into the subjectivity of self?

The idea of a fundamental unity of mind and matter figured in those debates; and that idea was associated with Spinoza. However, Spinoza's own treatment of the unity of mind and matter was in fact very different from what was offered in Romantic idealism. He would not have accepted the view of the world which Hegel, in his *Lectures on the History of Philosophy*, later attributed to Schelling. On that model, the world is seen as a unified structure in which thought or spirit differs from matter, not in kind, but only in degree of development. For Spinoza, they are radically different – irreducible, yet nonetheless integrated through the unity of God-as-substance.

Let us turn now to the details of Spinoza's treatment of God and Nature. Famously and notoriously, his philosophy identified them. What exactly that startling identification amounts to is somewhat more difficult for today's readers to determine. Spinoza played – consciously, and at times ironically – with the ancient concept of substance to come up with his own way of thinking of God.

Spinoza's version of God has proved both fascinating and outrageous – in his own times and throughout the later history of philosophical thought. His talk of *Deus-sive-Natura* – God-or-Nature – is accompanied by other sets of concepts and distinctions which give it some continuity with more familiar versions of God, while also deeply unsettling them. It is also true that, though the Nature side of his equation is in some respects familiar, it is in other ways radically different.

Spinoza's God

Spinoza's identification of God and Nature is not complete. The God of his philosophy – in this respect, like that of many other philosophies – is infinite being. Like at least some of those other gods, its infinity is construed in terms of many attributes. However, Spinoza's God is infinite under an infinity of his version of attributes. 'By God I understand a being absolutely infinite, i.e., a substance consisting of an infinity of attributes, of which each one expresses an eternal and infinite essence' (EID6).

That notion of an infinity of divine attributes may resonate with more familiar beliefs in a God whose being is inexhaustible – rich beyond any comparison with the world in which its creatures have their being. Yet it is difficult to reconcile with Spinoza's apparent equation of God with Nature. If what is now thought of as Nature is to be construed as infinite, that seems to involve only infinitely more of the same – not an infinity of ways in which it might be what it is.

Another respect in which Spinoza's God may seem at first sight to resemble more familiar gods is that the richness of its being is said to be not fully captured in human knowing. Yet, in the case of Spinoza's God, there is a very different basis for this lack of accessibility. Though infinite under an infinity of attributes, this God is knowable under only two of them: thought and what Spinoza calls extension, which can for our purposes here be rendered adequately enough as matter. (It will become clear later that, although the term 'extension' has for Spinoza strong geometrical connotations; his version of extended material reality also emphasises dynamic 'forces for existing', associated with one of his central concepts, *conatus*.)

Under each of its attributes, Spinoza's God-or-substance has multiple modifications – modes. Under the attribute of thought, the modes of substance are what Spinoza calls ideas. This distinctive way of locating thought within the metaphysical categories of substance, attribute and mode shapes Spinoza's version of human reason.

The category terms Spinoza invokes here are familiar from earlier philosophical systems. However, in his usage, they operate in unfamiliar ways. There is but one substance – identified with God. Thought is here not a distinguishing feature of one kind of substance among others. It is one of an infinity of attributes, each of which totally 'expresses' the being of the one unique substance. There is, for Spinoza, no diversity of substances. 'In Nature there exists only one substance, and . . . it is absolutely infinite' (EIP10Schol.).

Spinoza insists that thought and extension both apply equally and fully to his version of God. Hence for him it is no less true to describe this substance as materially extended than it is to describe it as thinking. Immediately, this challenges a common way of thinking of God – as a supernatural being. For Spinoza, material extension is not something separate from God; it is one of its infinite attributes.

Spinoza thus rejects all versions of Creation that present the material world as produced by a non-material thinking thing. Yet he repudiates also any suggestion that this material substance can be treated as one corporeal body among others. For that would be to impose an impossible limitation on its infinite being.

Mind and matter are not all there is to Spinoza's God. What then is to be made of his talk of all those other divine attributes, which – unlike thought and extension – are inaccessible to human knowledge? This is no ordinary divine inaccessibility. It is not a restriction on the power of human knowing to reach something construed as supernatural. Whatever exists is for Spinoza wholly knowable – yet only under those two attributes: thought and extension.

In Spinoza's system, there are no mysteries that remain impenetrable – no transcendent or supernatural realm, beyond the limits of the natural world, and hence inaccessible to the powers of a human mind. The limitations Spinoza imposes on human reason do not arise from its restricted powers of knowing – as if some superior knower might do better. The confinement to thought and extension arises rather from the very nature of what it is to be a human mind. It is not just impossible that a human mind could have access to some other attribute of substance; it is unthinkable. An individual mind is itself a mode of substance – under the attribute of thought. Thus construed, thought has as its object extension, and nothing else.

On the account which Spinoza will go on to elaborate in *Ethics II*, a human mind is a mode of thought which has as its direct object a specific human body. 'The object of the idea constituting the human Mind is the Body, or a certain mode of Extension which actually exists, and nothing else' (EIIP13). That inherent connection with body cannot be set aside in any way which would allow the mind to have access also to some other of the infinite number of attributes of God-as-substance.

Human minds and bodies are thus for Spinoza not different kinds of thing inhabiting different parts of a shared totality, within which they might causally interact. In terms of more recent philosophical debates, Spinoza is neither a 'dualist' nor a 'materialist'. For him, minds and bodies are not reducible in either direction. They have equal status – as finite modes or modifications of substance under the attributes of thought or matter, respectively. Yet minds and bodies are united by the noncausal relation of idea to object, which holds across the difference between modes of those attributes.

Spinoza's repositioning of the mental and the physical as two attributes, under which the one substance is fully expressed, brings a radical shift in the construal of human knowledge. Bertrand Russell articulated something of the strangeness of this reorientation in a quizzical observation in his *Lectures on Logical Atomism*, first published in 1918. We should, he says, be cautious about thinking that all that exists is either mind or matter:

> One should always remember Spinoza's infinite attributes of Deity. It is likely that there are in the world the analogues of his infinite attributes. We have no acquaintance with them, but

there is no reason to suppose that the mental and the physical exhaust the whole universe... You do not know enough about the world for that.[9]

Russell may well have intended that remark mischievously. His own formulation of the point evokes a division of the one world into the mental, the physical and other things that are in principle knowable – though as yet unknown. That restriction on what is known falls short of the radical character of Spinoza's own articulation. Yet the novelty of the thought that the mental and the physical might not 'exhaust the whole universe' does capture something of the depth of Spinoza's challenge to familiar ways of thinking.

The unknowability of those other attributes of Spinoza's God is not due to there being some things in the world whose nature is as yet unknown. If thought and matter do not 'exhaust the whole universe', that for Spinoza is not because there are constituents of the one world that are neither material nor mental. It is, rather, because there is an infinity of other ways in which the whole of reality can be fully expressed.

Spinoza's treatment of human knowing does not merely unsettle confidence in what that knowing can at present reach. It also challenges something so familiar that it may be barely noticed – an underlying model of what it is to know at all: the construal of a mind as shaping up to a reality external to its own being.

There is more going on here than scepticism about the current limits of knowledge. Spinoza's additional attributes – towards which Russell playfully gestures – are not to be construed as in principle discoverable by some future human inquiry. Rather, they would be radically different ways of construing reality – ways in principle unthinkable by minds whose very being consists in being 'ideas of body'.

---

[9] Russell 2010: 60.

Spinoza's 'Nature'

As it occurs in Spinoza's philosophy, Nature comes in two forms: *Natura Naturans* and *Natura Naturata* – commonly rendered in English, somewhat awkwardly, as 'Nature Naturing' and 'Nature Natured'. The distinction is between the productive power of God-or-substance and the realisation of that power in the multiplicity of its modes. However, in Spinoza's version of God, there is no unrealised potentiality. So the two forms of *Natura* are inseparable. There is no realm of unrealised 'possibles', lying beyond the actual world. Where there is *Natura Naturans*, there too is *Natura Naturata*.

Something of Spinoza's *Natura Naturata* resonates in the modern understanding of Nature as the totality of the 'natural' world. What he calls *Natura Naturans* is less easy to accommodate. It is the power of Nature, as distinct from the products of that power. Yet this power is not construed as an external causal force, exerted by a Creator. It is a pervasive presence throughout the totality of finite things. Both senses of *Natura* are at play, as we will see, throughout Spinoza's treatment of human thought and its relations with the rest of the world.

The sense of 'Nature' that is common in contemporary discourse, and that involved in Spinoza's *Natura Naturata*, are readily intelligible in terms of one another. Yet there are some tensions between them. Those tensions surface in the familiar, though by no means straightforward, distinction between human and nonhuman parts of Nature, which tends to centre on the human capacity for reason.

At a superficial level, it may seem trite to point out that human knowers are themselves part of the reality they seek to know. Human beings know that their bodies are part of the natural world. They also readily acknowledge that their minds are also part of that reality. For the most part, they do not seriously think of themselves as positioned outside the world like observing gods, viewing it from everywhere – or, perhaps more strangely, from nowhere. Yet human knowing is readily imagined as a relation between a mind, complete unto itself, and a world of things external to it – including its own body.

Spinoza challenges that familiar way of imagining human knowing. He demands of his readers that they engage seriously with the ramifications of seeing themselves as embodied minds-in-world – encompassed within the totality of finite modes, and seeking understanding from within that totality.

There is no one simple opposition at stake in the relations between reason and Nature that played out in post-Kantian idealism and in Romanticism. The celebration of a 'sublime discord' within reason was not directed against the notion of 'rational order' in Nature. The Romantics were not anti-science. Yet Romanticism – as a literary and cultural movement – did challenge what it saw as the stifling rigidity of thought processes extolled under the name of reason. Spinoza's affirmation of the integration of reason, imagination and emotion – of which we will see more later – was one of the strands in his thought that strongly appealed to Romantic sensibility.

Romantic idealism, in the wake of Kant, offered what was in some ways an imaginative rethinking of some aspects of Spinoza's philosophy – not all of which were clearly understood. Much of that idealism was in fact alien to Spinoza's metaphysics. Hence, to read Spinoza now can be to rediscover ways of thinking of human relations with the rest of Nature which preceded Romanticism. Yet it is also the case that Romanticism was itself influenced by a misunderstanding of his views.

To see what was unusual in Spinoza's treatment of the relations between human minds and Nature, it is helpful to look briefly at how those relations were seen by one of his contemporaries, whose thoughts also resonate in contemporary attitudes towards Nature. The idea of reason's supremacy over mere Nature did not come from Spinoza. Yet its possibility was articulated by one of his near contemporaries, Blaise Pascal.

The Feeling of Immensity

Reflecting, in his *Pensées*, on the immensity of the world, Pascal – like Spinoza – stressed the interconnections that bind finite things to one another. For Pascal that meant that a mind could not clearly know either itself or anything else; he saw the parts of the whole as so interconnected that no one of them could be known without knowing all the others. That suggests a bleak prognosis for human reason, striving to understand Nature. It also suggests an extreme vulnerability of human beings in the face of the overwhelming strength of non-human parts of the whole.

Famously, Pascal went on to depict a human being as the weakest thing in Nature – like a fragile reed, so weak that it takes something far less than the combined strength of all that is non-human to crush it. 'A vapour, a drop of water, is enough to kill him.'[10] Nor is that the worst of it. Contemplating the whole of Nature, Pascal continues, we realise that the entire Earth is itself a mere speck. Compared to the orbits of the stars, the whole visible world is only an imperceptible dot; and even that is not a secure fixed spot: nothing stands still for us.

Faced with the dire insignificance of that speck of human life in infinite space, Pascal's thoughts turn to the brief span of his own life – its very existence swallowed up in immensity. The silence of those infinite spaces, he says, fills him with dread. Moving on from that dread, however, Pascal's thinking takes a turn that is dramatically different from Spinoza's treatment of the immersion of human minds into the immense totality of being.

That shift in the trajectory of Pascal's reflections reverberates in later post-Kantian thought on reason's connections with the sublime. 'Through space', Pascal says, 'the universe grasps me and swallows me up like a speck; through thought I grasp it.'[11] Even if the universe were to crush him, he concludes, a human being would still be nobler than the rest of Nature: for this fragile reed is unique in being a reed that thinks.

For Pascal the fragility of a human being within the whole of Nature is encompassed – and compensated – by the possession of reason, which he sees as a gift from a God who transcends Nature. Within that theological frame, pride in being thus distinguished from the rest of Nature is offset by humility before the supernatural. Within the very different frame of Spinoza's rejection of the supernatural, a mind's finding ease and contentment within

---

[10] Pascal 1996: 95.
[11] Ibid. 59 (Sec. V, fragment 113).

the immensity of the whole of Nature must follow a different trajectory.

In a remark which sounds similar to Pascal's reflections on the human predicament, Spinoza observes, in Chapter 16 of his *Theological-Political Treatise*, that reason is itself a mere speck within the totality of being:

> Nature is not constrained by the laws of human reason, which aim only at man's true advantage and preservation. It is governed by infinite other laws, which look to the eternal order of the whole of nature, of which man is only a small part.[12]

Yet there is no suggestion in Spinoza's philosophy that the possession of reason might nonetheless make a human being superior to, or dominant over, the immensity of the whole.

Pascal presented the human mind as humbled before a God whose being transcended all natural things. It would be misleading to suggest that he saw human thought as empowered to rightly dominate Nature. Nor did he endorse the supremacy of reason within the human mind over other aspects of mental life. He famously observed that 'the heart has its reasons of which reason knows nothing'.[13] Yet it is possible to see some affinities between Pascal's reflections on the nobility of the reed that thinks and later exalted self-satisfaction in the supposed supremacy of reason over the rest of Nature.

We will see later that Spinoza, throughout the *Ethics*, offers his own version of a human mind's gaining release from the 'bondage' of subjection to non-human powers. It involves a distinctive treatment of the nature of human freedom, in which he insists that human beings do not hold any privileged position within the necessities that bind the whole of Nature. Although Spinoza is now often read through the lens of later developments in Romantic idealism, his version of reason offers a very different understanding of the relations between human and non-human powers.

---

[12] Curley 2016: 284.
[13] Pascal 1996: 154 (fragment 423).

Reason and Nature

The notion of the sublime lingers in contemporary aesthetic appreciation of areas of Nature associated with the non-human. It can be discerned in the celebration of wilderness, untamed by human presence. There are echoes of Romanticism in some of the rhetoric of later environmentalism, centred on ideals of conservation or restoration of unspoiled Nature.

Those post-Romantic connotations of 'Nature' coexist with the residue of very different connotations of the term, which come from older philosophical ways of thinking of the natural world, which are also echoed in the *Ethics*. They are epitomised in the idea of laws of Nature, governing universal necessities.

The notion of a rational order of things, reflected in laws of Nature, fits neatly with seeing the natural world as produced by a supernatural Creator. However, Spinoza rejected all reference to purposeful design as the basis for the universal necessities of the world. He makes it clear in *Ethics I* that his God-or-substance is not a Creator, located beyond Nature. Nor is it to be regarded as a transcendent knower, apprehending the totality of things from a position somehow beyond them all. Instead, he offers his non-purposeful God-as-substance – totally and necessarily expressed under attributes, of which thought and matter are two.

In rejecting the supernatural, Spinoza construes humanity in a different configuration with Nature. Rather than being the antithesis of Nature, human beings are included in a totality of finite modes – subject to the same necessities that govern all. Their capacity for reason is a human power within that totality, struggling to persist amid the powers of other finite beings. That power of reason is not construed in terms of a God-given dominance over the rest of Nature.

The *Ethics* elaborates the ramifications of a tantalising conjunction: a powerful celebration of the distinctive powers of human minds, together with a firm denial that those powers involve a privileged position of supremacy over the non-human. Clearly, such an approach to the relations between human and non-human within the totality of Nature held considerable appeal in the context of twentieth-century environmental concerns. From the

1970s, philosophers who shared those concerns looked to Spinoza as a source of insights into how better to conceptualise resistance to prevailing cultural assumptions about human supremacy over the non-human.

Spinoza and Environmental Philosophy

A central theme in late twentieth-century Environmental Philosophy was the critique of 'human exceptionalism' – the supposed special status of human beings in the natural world. A major thread in that critique concerned the potential of ideas drawn from ecology for rethinking the relations between human and non-human; the very concept of 'ecology' involved their interconnection.

Out of increased understanding of the broader ramifications of ecological studies, came a new emphasis on the cultivation of 'ecological attitudes' towards human presence in the world. It was to this ecological strand in Environmental Philosophy that Spinoza's philosophy, with its emphasis on the interconnection of modes in a totality, became significant. It gained visibility especially through the pioneering work of the Norwegian philosopher Arne Næss, who observed: 'No great philosopher has so much to offer in the way of clarification and articulation of basic ecological attitudes as Baruch Spinoza'.[14]

Central to Næss's articulation of those 'ecological attitudes' was a distinction between 'shallow' and 'deep' ecology. His own philosophical thinking had followed a remarkable trajectory – from early associations with the logical empiricism of the Vienna Circle, and early scholarly interest in Spinozist metaphysics, to his work in 'ecophilosophy' in the 1970s. He continued to refine that work through later decades, absorbing, and adapting to his own use, insights from developments in feminist philosophy and postmodern theory.

Næss's distinction between 'the shallow' and 'the deep' was presented in a lecture at the World Future Research Conference, in Bucharest in 1972. On his account, the 'shallow' ecologi-

[14] Næss 1977: 54.

cal movement, which was current at the time, was oriented to human-centred concerns – primarily pollution and resource depletion. In contrast, he saw the emerging 'deep' ecology movement as directed away from the image of 'man-in-environment' towards a more relational 'total field' image of interconnected life forces.[15]

In retrospect, it is striking that Næss's distinction was originally drawn as a contrast between ecological movements. It reflected a political concern that a narrow focus on resistance to pollution and resource depletion might gain traction – to the detriment of less human-centred ecological harms. Næss was also directly concerned with critique of trends in decision processes in the funding of scientific research.

Næss's efforts in the 1970s to 'deepen' the conceptualisation of 'ecological attitudes' were prescient in relation to the then future politics of climate change. He was already sketching the implications of different ways of imagining human presence in Nature. He talked in his Bucharest lecture of moving away from a master–slave model to alternative ways of thinking of human–non-human relations, stressing shared interests or 'species-partnerships'.

Those early insights on 'deep ecology' resonate in Næss's later theorising of interspecies relations. What is even more significant, in the context of contemporary experience and response to climate change, is his prescience in emphasising, at that early stage, an emerging complexity in the understanding of 'organisms, ways of life, and interactions in the biosphere in general'. It all indicated, he observed, the need for 'a keen, steady perception of the profound human ignorance of biospherical relationships and therefore of the effect of disturbances'.[16]

In the 1970s, Næss was already looking to a wider ecophilosophical orientation of his version of 'deep ecology' – to the development of something akin to 'a system of the kind instanced by Aristotle or Spinoza'.[17] Though what followed was not really akin to such a philosophical system, 'deep ecology' did set the

[15] Næss 1973.
[16] Ibid. 5.
[17] Ibid. 7.

scene for a range of further attempts to relate Spinoza to current environmental issues.

There were crossed wires – and conflicted purposes – in the philosophical literature that ensued. Concern with how best to think interspecies relations was caught up with related, yet differently based, interest in ethical issues arising at the time around human treatment of animals. Concern with animal rights and the conceptual ramifications of ecology were of course inter-related through a common concern with interspecies relations. Yet there were also some tensions between the two sets of issues; and the figure of Spinoza became a focal point for those tensions.

The apparent ease with which Spinoza could be drafted into contemporary ecophilosophy was, on the face of it, at odds with some explicit observations in the *Ethics* about the sentimentality of laws or customs that resisted the mistreatment of animals. Contemporary issues around the extension of juridical concepts of rights competed for attention with the broader affinities of Spinoza's philosophy with conceptual aspects of ecology. The positive appeal of his emphasis on interconnection was in tension with the countervailing negativity of his explicit prioritising of the needs and interests of fellow humans over the well-being of non-human species.

In later years, those issues were disentangled – allowing a clearer view of how exactly Spinoza's philosophy, including elements of his political philosophy, might be brought to bear on understanding the relations between human and non-human on a changing planet. Hasana Sharp's *Spinoza and the Politics of Renaturalization*, published in 2011, offered an insightful analysis of cross-currents in those earlier debates of the late twentieth century.

Sharp argued that the rationale of Spinoza's troubling remarks about other species had little to do with issues of animal cruelty or exploitation. Rather, his primary target was a way of valuing animals – current in his own time – which involved a devaluing of human beings. On Sharp's account, Spinoza's main concern was with criticising those who romanticise 'brutish' existence, thereby disparaging humanity.[18]

---

[18] Sharp 2011. See especially Chapter 6, 'Nature, Norms, and Beasts', pp. 185–220.

As Sharp noted, in more recent times the term 'human' appears in a markedly different landscape; human–non-human alienation has become a greater risk than human–animal identification. What may be added to that, from a later perspective, is that Spinoza's affirmation of the strengths of human community remain relevant amid accelerated climate change.

There can be an element of misanthropy in some forms of 'environmentalism' which tend to present the human species as of itself a destructive force within Nature. Spinoza's philosophy, in contrast, offers a joyous affirmation of human presence in Nature, while also yielding a basis for the recognition of those destructive forms of social organisation that act to the detriment of humans and non-human alike.

In retrospect, Næss was right to insist on the powerful potential of Spinoza's philosophy for a future ecophilosophy – notwithstanding Spinoza's own distrust of what he saw as a sentimental preferencing of animals over humans. Yet the Environmental Philosophy of the late twentieth century – despite its critique of 'human exceptionalism' – had its own undercurrents of unexamined human-centredness.

Concern with 'the environment' may seek to shift focus from human to non-human. Yet the concept itself implicitly centres the totality around humanity. Næss himself later reflected on the oddity of contrasting an ecological standpoint with an anthropocentric one. From an ecological standpoint, he asked, 'is my attention, concern, respect, valuation, really centered on the ecosystems, the biosphere as a whole, the planet earth?'[19]

It is, nonetheless, undeniable that twentieth-century Environmental Philosophy prefigured later intellectual developments in the context of climate change. It stimulated broader concern with the metaphysics of interconnection. Its insights resonate also in more recent ideas of the biosphere as 'self-realising', which have continuity with Næss's earlier articulations of Spinozist 'ecological attitudes'.[20]

---

[19] Næss 1999: 419.
[20] For an account of the role of Deep Ecology, and its limitations, in relation to later discussion of 'self-realisation', with reference to Spinoza, see

Conceptual issues about anthropocentricity have arisen around contemporary responses to climate change. Those issues take on a new urgency amid the interconnected crises of global warming and virus transmission across species. The destruction of habitat in exploitation of 'natural' resources; the encroachment of animal species into hitherto 'human' domains; the impact of ocean warming and expanded commercial fishing on food security: all those issues cluster around increasingly porous borders between 'human' and 'non-human'.

Reading Spinoza in this context can have wider import than concern with human treatment of animals. It can be brought to bear on how best to imagine the relations between 'human' and 'non-human' within Nature.

Human, Non-human and the 'More than Human'

Some aspects of human concern with the well-being of other species can be readily accommodated without abandoning the mindset of human supremacy within Nature. That mentality can readily coexist with recognising relations of sympathetic connection and collaboration between human and other species, in settings which are explicitly human-centred – as in relations with 'domestic' animals. Grasping the complexities of interspecies relations in the wild can, in contrast, involve deep and destabilising shifts in thought.

Assumptions of human supremacy are shaken by increased understanding of non-human intelligence, on display in the adaptation of non-human species to habitat; and in their capacities to interact with other species in a changing environment. Yet outdated assumptions often linger in the ways in which new factual knowledge is articulated.

Knowing that an octopus can use its tentacles to open a jar, or that a bird can use a stick as a tool, can induce wonder at their ingenuity. Such performances offer unexpected manifestations of human-like manipulation or calculation – perhaps enhanced, in

Mathews 2021, especially Chapter 4, Sections 5 and 6. *The Ecological Self* was first published in 1991.

the case of the octopus, by the physical advantages associated with extra arms. Human observers are more readily impressed by what seems an exceptional performance by a gifted individual animal than by manifestations of previously unknown capacities in non-human species. That selective wonder can carry an unexamined assumption that the intelligence of other species is to be measured in terms of the capacity to demonstrate human-like dexterity or deliberation.

Animal intelligence is commonly judged with reference to a human norm, eliding the relations between species and the environments in which their capacities and powers have been shaped. Assumptions underlying that judgement become more visible when the focus shifts from individual performances to the exercise of collective intelligence. Regular patterns of migration; relocations from depleted habitat; exploitation of the presence of other species: such displays are more challenging to familiar assumptions of human supremacy than individual performances, viewed in abstraction from environment.

The eliding of environmental context helps explain the frequent resort to talk of 'blind' or 'mindless' instinct, when describing the behaviour of non-human species. Strong borders operate in common understanding of intelligent behaviour – even if some porousness may be allowed in the case of animal behaviours that seem to imitate human skills, or approximate to human powers. There is a general reluctance to shed human supremacy, even in the face of confrontation with the awe-inspiring collective intelligence of non-human species. The assumption persists that only what is human-like fully warrants the ascription of mind or thought.

In trying to shift habitual mindsets, some scientifically informed advocates for climate change action have adopted a locution of 'the more than human'. The locution is meant to shake human-centred assumptions, conveying a deeper appreciation of the interdependence of species. Lesley Head, in *Hope and Grief in the Anthropocene*, published in 2016, explains the locution as acknowledging 'both the pervasiveness of human influence and its interaction with non-humans (plants, animals, rocks, weather)'.[21]

---

[21] Head 2016: 56.

Rather than being the centre around which all else revolves, what is human is here reconstrued as one among other interdependent forms of being.

This rhetorical strategy challenges the assumed centrality of human presence in Nature. It refigures humankind as one among other species – though one that is also capable of wreaking harm on the interdependent whole. However, the decentring also opens up further unresolved questions about human presence in that shared domain. Where does the human fit within this new space of the 'more than human'? Is it one among others, or first among equals? And is human thought itself to be included in the more-than-human totality?

Spinoza's treatment of God and Nature has ramifications which can be brought to bear on those questions. It can help clarify what is at stake in contemporary attempts to rethink narratives of human supremacy. In the next chapter we will see how, in *Ethics II*, he applies his metaphysics of substance, attributes and modes to develop a distinctive account of human knowing as inherently embodied, and hence inextricably immersed within the whole of Nature.

Central to the structure of *Ethics II* – and ultimately to the whole work – is Spinoza's rejection of a rival philosophical account of knowledge, truth and error, associated with the philosophy of Descartes. That Cartesian way of thinking of human knowing remains familiar, and intuitively appealing, in current times – despite the receding of the philosophical doctrine of 'dualism', along with theological assumptions that sustained Descartes's model in its historical context.

2
Embodied Knowing

The legacy of the Cartesian conceptualising of human thought lingers in Western consciousness; it can seem the natural way of thinking of the presence of minds in the world. In the original model, as offered by Descartes, a self-contained individual thinking substance apprehends ideas – mental objects arrayed before it, awaiting judgement. Those mental items are construed as derived from non-mental things in the material world, which act causally on the mind. The mind inspects them to determine whether they carry distinguishing marks of truth; its faculty of will then gives or withholds assent.

Belief in minds as separate entities, utterly different in kind from matter, has receded with the demise of Cartesian dualism as a philosophical theory of mind–body relations. Yet the Cartesian model of human knowing, which Spinoza subjected to scathing criticism, has persisted in collective imagination – despite the gradual disintegration of the philosophical and theological apparatus which supported it. Human minds – whatever their relations with human brains – are still readily construed as holding a privileged position, around which the rest of Nature is configured.

The dualism of mind and matter, which has been repudiated in more recent philosophical critiques of Descartes, has lingered in the imagining of human relations with Nature. Even current calls for a more integrative view of those relations are often couched in terms of improved human adaptation or adjustment to material Nature – as if two separable domains are now to be brought into a new alignment.

Spinoza's model of embodiment within the totality of things disrupts the habitual imagining of human minds as having an external perspective on Nature. The assumed special status of minds is so familiar that it tends to go unnoticed. Yet it can obfuscate insight into the ramifications of climate change. In offering an alternative model of human knowing, Spinoza's philosophy – read in this new context – can help clarify the tensions in contemporary ways of thinking of the relations between human and non-human.

Imagining Human and Non-human

Talk of the 'more than human' in contemporary climate change discussion is often associated with a search for appropriate metaphors to capture cross-species relations and interactions, bringing together the literal and the figurative. Scientifically informed observations of interactions across species are often articulated in terms drawn from human interactions.

A science journalist has speculated that a dense glade of cypress trees can be seen as a 'single organism – communicating, socialising and supporting itself via an intricate web of hidden roots and fungal filaments, conspiracies of insects and the chemistry of scent'. In that description, the language of 'communication' is not merely fanciful. It reflects contemporary research, directed to understanding actual subterranean interactions happening within species of trees, as if in a 'coded language'.[1]

Metaphors can capture real interconnections – not just imaginary ones – across divisions between forms of life. Nor is the articulation of commonalities confined to direct comparisons with the human species. The ecological richness of submarine kelp zones has prompted descriptions drawn from more familiar interweaving of plant, tree and animal life within the familiar unity of a forest – evoking a similar sense of threatened reciprocal thriving among different species.[2]

---

[1] Chandler 2020: 64.
[2] Ryan 2020: 189.

There are complex mixtures of literal and figurative language involved in such communication of interconnection. It is human observers that notice resemblances between areas of ocean kelp and a forest – or between forests and human social collectivities. More generally, it is from the perspective of human observation, using categories drawn from human thought, that commonalities are grasped.

Detachment from, and immersion within, the natural world, are both at play in those observations. In some situations an actual first-hand observer might be literally immersed in a figurative submarine 'forest', without thinking of themselves as part of the reality of that complex array of organisms. They might be astonished to realise that they are indeed thus positioned within a realm of non-human interconnection, potentially disrupted by their presence. Not all human perceptions of non-human species are, in that literal sense, 'immersed'. Yet human understanding of the non-human involves an inherently human framing.

Contemporary talk of the 'the more than human', in the context of climate change, is suffused by human imagining, without thereby forfeiting scientific objectivity. The locution, after all, has largely originated from actual scientific observation of species-in-environment. Yet the framing is itself unavoidably human. It is from an authoritative human perspective that the interdependence of human and non-human is articulated.

Human thought retains authority in descriptions of what is non-human. It judges the appropriateness of metaphors, determines their limits and adjusts emotional response to requirements of objectivity. To acknowledge that implicit authoritative positioning of the human does not undermine the rhetorical strategy involved in talk of the 'more than human'. It does, however, highlight the role of human imagination in articulating truths of interdependence.

Spinoza's treatment of human knowing can help clarify this implicit human framing, which can operate in the very act of denying human supremacy within Nature. Engaging with his philosophy can offer insight into how the framing operates – not in order to avoid it, but in order to better understand its nature and its implications. It can make it easier to see that there are in fact two very different ways of being 'centred' on the human.

On the one hand, there is a relatively innocuous anthropomorphising in human understanding of the non-human. Seen through a Spinozist lens, that is a feature of the way human minds work – understanding from within the totality of being. In contrast, there is a distorting anthropocentric construal of the non-human, which gives human minds the status of beings complete unto themselves, which hold a privileged position in the whole.

There are truths now known about the interconnections of species and environments which were unavailable to Spinoza. Yet reading him now can yield a conceptual basis for rejecting false assumptions of anthropocentrism, while yet mindfully acknowledging the anthropomorphising inherent in a mind's effort to understand itself within the whole of Nature. Insights drawn from his philosophy may thus help sustain and strengthen insights into wholeness – akin to what Arne Næss called 'ecological attitudes' – which can encompass the reciprocal thriving of human and non-human under the threats posed by climate change.

However, it is not just thought about human thought's relations with the rest of Nature that undergoes a shift in Spinoza's alternative to the Cartesian model. It is the very understanding of what it is for human minds to think at all; and of what it is for them to think truly about anything. The metaphysical definitions in *Ethics I* are crucial to understanding both Spinoza's treatment of mind–body relations, and his account of human knowing, in *Ethics II*.

In Spinoza's terminology, God-or-substance is completely 'expressed' both as extension and as thought. Under the attribute of extension, that expression yields the totality of finite material things. Under the attribute of thought, the expression of substance also yields a totality of finite modes – ideas. Because each totality expresses the whole being of substance, there is nothing expressed under the one attribute that is not also expressed under the other. The completeness in the expression of substance under its attributes means that there can be no causal relations between human minds and bodies. They are, nonetheless related – across the difference of attributes – as ideas to the objects of those ideas.

Spinoza offers a radically different alternative to Descartes's treatment of human knowing, and to his accounts of the nature of truth and error. Attending to the detail of some of the arguments in *Ethics II* can yield insight into the important role Spinoza gave imagination in human knowing, and into how that might now assist better understanding the relations between human and non-human.

Human Knowing and the Good Life

Spinoza's differences from Descartes on the nature of human knowing emerge most starkly in their different approaches to scepticism and certainty. Here, the crucial role of imagination in Spinoza's philosophy becomes apparent. It also emerges that his concern with human knowing is much deeper than merely having the correct epistemological theory.

For Descartes, notoriously, there is a serious question as to whether a human mind can know that it knows. In the Fifth of his *Meditations*, after painstaking argumentation, he resolves that question in the affirmative: a mind can indeed have certainty – provided it goes in the right way about the business of knowing. A human mind should exercise its free will in granting or withholding assent in relation to the ideas that come before it, in accordance with criteria of 'clearness' and 'distinctness'.[3] For Spinoza, throughout Part II of the *Ethics*, there is no problem in knowing that we know. Truth, he insists, provides its own standard. Indubitability resides in the very act of knowing, without appeal to marks of truth.

To a committed sceptic, this dismissal of the supposed problem of certainty may well seem sheer dogmatism. Whereas Descartes takes scepticism seriously – even if only in order to refute it – Spinoza insists there is no problem to begin with. Faced with his repeated dismissal of sceptical doubt, modern readers may well have some sympathy with the perspective of a disgruntled sceptic. However, there is much more going on here than a skirmish between competing theories in epistemology. Spinoza's rejection

[3] Descartes 1984: 48–9.

of Cartesian certainty hinges on a denial of the distinction between intellect and will within the human mind. Hence, his version of knowledge is bound up with a more notorious thread in his philosophy: the denial of free will, on which he builds his treatment of the real nature of freedom, and of the well-lived human life.

Spinoza makes explicit, towards the end of *Ethics II*, his deeper agenda in rejecting Descartes's model of error. It has consequences, he claims, for understanding how best to live. He promises to discuss those consequences more fully in later sections of *Ethics*. Meanwhile, he assures his readers that his rejection of the Cartesian model of knowing is 'quite necessary' – not only for the sake of theoretical speculation, but also 'in order to arrange one's life wisely' (EIIP49Schol.II).

For Spinoza what is at stake here is understanding the deep truth of what human minds are. That is, in turn, the key to living well. What may seem at first sight to be only an argument between philosophers about certainty is, in fact, something much deeper – a conflicted understanding of the nature of human thought, which goes to the heart of human existence. The whole story unfolds from Spinoza's repudiation of the notion of free will, around which Descartes had built both his now-familiar version of human knowing and his influential construal of human presence in Nature.

Descartes's treatment of knowledge, truth and error is framed by belief in a supernatural Creator, in whom will is distinct from intellect – a distinction which is mirrored in the creation of human minds. Spinoza's treatment of the human mind is framed by his radically different construal of God – as a unique substance, which is both thinking and extended, and in which there is no distinction between will and intellect.

As if in riposte to Descartes's theological framing of human knowing, Spinoza argues throughout the *Ethics* that human minds share in the divine nature; and that they do so the more they understand themselves. Hence, in the human mind there is no distinction between will and intellect. Spinoza's rejection of that distinction shapes a radically different account of what it is to know, and of the nature of error.

Descartes's treatment of certainty in the *Meditations* draws out the implications of the way he positions human minds within the world. Famously, the resolution he offers of the 'problem' of human error relies on the benign nature of a transcendent, all-powerful, non-deceiving God. In that conceptual structure, certainty depends not only on human will but also on a divine will – acting purposefully for the ultimate well-being of human beings.

Descartes's model of truth and error is thus grounded in a way of thinking of the natural and the supernatural. He construes the relations of human error to truth along the lines of human sin's relation to goodness. In that respect, what some commentators have seen as Descartes's 'ethics of belief' – his recommendations on how best to go about knowing – is akin, not just to a theory of ethics, but to a theodicy.

For Descartes, the 'problem' is how to explain – and hence how to avoid – human error. His solution is to cast error as resulting from a misuse of free will, akin to its misuse in sin. He offers not just an explanation of this apparent aberration, but a justification of its existence. On this approach, error has its place in a world made by a benign Creator, just as sin does. Their problematic existence can be understood by appeal to the workings of divine and human will. For Descartes, the possibility of error – like the possibility of sin – is the other side of the coin to the gift of free will, which a loving Creator has bestowed on human beings.

In elaborating this account of human error in the Fourth of his *Meditations*, Descartes observes that the human will is able to reach beyond the range of the human intellect. A mind can exercise its will wrongly, in assenting to the supposed truth of what its intellect does not clearly and distinctly understand. He sees the range of a human will as resembling, in that respect, the infinite range of the divine will. Though it is finite, the operation of a human will can range beyond its understanding.[4]

Descartes's emphasis on the possible misuse of the human will is one among other points in his argumentation where there are echoes of Augustine's treatment of God's relations with the created world. There is some irony, then, in Spinoza's insistence that a human mind is not merely made in resemblance of the mind of a supernatural God. For him a human mind is itself part of a

[4] Descartes 1984: 39–40.

non-supernatural God-or-Nature, in which there is no distinction between will and intellect.

For Spinoza the possibility of error does not arise from an aberration; it is inherent in a human mind's immersion in the totality of the world. As we will see in more detail shortly, error is for him ontologically based in the metaphysics of substance and finite modes. Hence, access to truth and proneness to error must both be understood in terms of the interdependence of a mind's own powers with those of other things – all encompassed within a totality, in which the being of substance is completely expressed.

On Spinoza's diagnosis, Descartes was thus responsible for a deep error about human knowledge, related to his crediting human beings with a freely acting will. According to Spinoza, that underlying illusion of free will reflects a mistaken picture of humanity as occupying a privileged domain within Nature. It involves seeing human beings as lodged within the world as if they inhabit a kingdom within a kingdom – exempt from the necessities that govern the rest of Nature.

For Spinoza, understanding what it is to know – and to live well as a human being – involves surrendering that distorted understanding of humanity's place in Nature. That is why he sees the key to understanding how to 'arrange one's life wisely' as insight into the interdependence of the powers of a human mind with the powers of all other finite things.

The Nature of Imagination

Descartes pictured human knowing as involving intellect's evaluation of ideas, which are themselves construed as passive mental items. The mind's inspection, directed to marks of truth, is followed by an act of affirmation or negation, performed by a freely acting will. On that picture, human minds have a God-given capacity to access truth, if only they follow the right procedure. That Cartesian model of human knowing accompanies a broader way of thinking of human presence in the world, which lingers in contemporary thought, though the supportive role played by its framing assumptions has receded.

In Spinoza's alternative account of human knowing there is a shift of focus – from the supposed role of human free will to a mind's interdependence within the totality of finite modes. Such a mind is what it is, and does what it does, only as included within the whole of Nature. That makes its proneness to inadequate knowing inevitable.

Crucial to the model of truth and error that Spinoza goes on to develop is his treatment of the nature of imagination. For him, its nature resides in a mind's felt awareness of a body – of which it is the idea – being affected by other bodies:

> If the human Body is affected with a mode that involves the nature of an external body, the human Mind will regard the same external body as actually existing, or as present to it, until the Body is affected by an [affection] that excludes the existence or presence of that body. (EIIP17)

He adds in a scholium that such 'affections' are to be called 'images of things'; and that when the mind regards bodies in this way, it 'imagines' (EIIP17Schol.).

Spinoza insists, nonetheless, that imagination is not of itself a source of error. Imaginings, considered in themselves, contain no error. In a tantalising observation, he adds that this will 'begin to indicate' what error is. 'The Mind does not err from the fact that it imagines, but only in so far as it is considered to lack an idea that excludes the existence of those things it imagines to be present to it' (EIIP17Schol.).

The human capacity to imagine is thus for Spinoza the basis – though not the cause – of human error. Significantly, that same capacity to imagine is the basis also of a human mind's capacity to form the 'common notions' of reason, through which the mind comes to more adequate understanding. A human mind is inherently prone to error. For it 'perceives the nature of a great many bodies together with the nature of its own body' (EIIP16Cor.1).

That proneness to error is only part of the story. The mind's efforts towards ever better understanding can be assisted, as well as impeded, by its interdependence with other finite modes. 'The Mind is the more capable of perceiving many things adequately as its Body has many things in common with other bodies' (*E*IIP39Cor.).

Spinoza's shifts between the consideration of free will and the consideration of imagination are central to grasping the upshot of his treatment of embodied knowing, in the context of contemporary climate change discourse. However, before considering its full implications, it is important to first see how he manages to reject the whole notion of free will, while yet maintaining the active power and freedom of the human mind within the totality of Nature.

Human Freedom and Spinoza's Conatus

A repudiation of free will may seem an unpromising start to a refiguration of human knowing in a contemporary context. Yet, in rejecting free will, Spinoza nonetheless affirms human freedom – while radically reconstruing it. He also retains Descartes's central emphasis on mental activity as the basis for access to truth, while offering a very different account of what that activity involves.

The activity that Descartes attributed to a freely acting human will, operating separately from intellect, is for Spinoza inherent in the very existence of an 'idea'. What is more, a human mind is itself an idea, actively engaged in the understanding of body – its object. It may at first seem paradoxical to both affirm a mind's free activity and insist that it is inserted into the necessities that govern the whole of Nature. Yet the details of Spinoza's defence of that conjunction open up possibilities for a radical rethinking of the nature of a human mind's presence in its world.

Spinoza's version of mental activity is closely associated with his central concept of 'conatus' – a dynamic striving to persist in being, which is essential to the existence of a finite mode. Human bodies – like all finite modes – strive for continued existence. For them, that involves the persistence of a specific proportion of motion and rest within the totality of finite modes of substance, expressed as extension.

A human mind is also a finite mode of substance, though under a different attribute – thought. Hence the mind has its own conatus, which consists in the effort to understand ever better the body of which it is the idea. This emphasis on a mind's inherent activity, as idea-of-body, reinforces Spinoza's repudiation of Descartes's model of ideas as like passive pictures.

For Spinoza, a mind's striving to understand is conceptually interconnected with – though distinguishable from – the conatus of the body of which it is the idea. Here, the relationship between the attributes – mind and matter – plays out at the level of individual minds and bodies. It is through his concept of conatus that Spinoza is able to capture the sense of mental activity which might otherwise seem to have gone missing from his treatment of human knowing. The activity which – on the Cartesian model – had to be added to an idea by a separate act of will, is for Spinoza inherent in the idea itself.

Descartes's account of human knowing reflected the assumption of a privileged positioning of human beings within the world – the model which Spinoza mocked as implying a territory exempt from necessities. Spinoza's own version of mental activity emphasises that the powers at stake in a mind's conatus are caught up with the interdependence of bodies within the totality of finite modes, affecting and being affected by one another. For Spinoza, a human mind, as idea of a particular body, reflects the fluctuations of interacting bodies. Its powers of acting are bound up with – though not causally determined by – the affections of the body of which it is the idea.

Looking at it all from outside Spinoza's metaphysics, it might seem that all this amounts to a limitation on a mind's powers, arising from its contingent connections with body. However, for Spinoza, it is only as idea-of-body that a human mind exists at all. It strives to persist in being – in understanding – only as embodied mind.

Human knowing is thus for Spinoza grounded in the status of minds as ideas of bodies affected by other bodies. A mind's striving to understand reflects felt awareness of a specific body which is interdependent with others. He articulates that grounding in felt awareness of body early in *Ethics II*, at Axiom 4: 'We *feel* that a certain body is affected in many ways' [my emphasis].

Spinoza's emphasis on the felt awareness of body may seem, of itself, to be at odds with affirming the power and autonomy of human reason. Yet he emphasises also the mind's freedom to act unimpeded – in accordance with its own powers, unrestrained by the contingency of ways in which its body happens to be affected. The coexistence of those two strands – autonomy and interdependence – yields a distinctive version of the power of human reason. We will see it recur later in the *Ethics* in his treatment of friendship, and in his treatment of human collectivities in his political writings.

Reason and Spinoza's God-or-Substance

Spinoza celebrates human reason, without endorsing its supremacy within the mind. On his account, the power of reason is exerted, not in suppressing imagination and emotion, but in its capacity to draw strength from interaction with them. The nuances of this version of reason as grounded in felt awareness of body resist classification in terms of either side of later philosophical oppositions between 'rationalism' and 'empiricism'.

Since a mind is, for Spinoza, itself an idea, it is of its own nature active. Yet its striving to understand is bound up with bodily powers, which are vulnerable to the rival powers of other material modes. Hence, it seems, a human mind is both subject to the necessities that govern the whole of Nature, and yet – in its own activity – free.

Spinoza embraces this apparent paradox as a feature of human thought. A human mind, despite its power of free activity, is also subject to passivities that reflect the fortuitous fluctuations of bodies. Resolving this apparent tension involves considering Spinoza's important distinction between ideas that can be understood through the mind's own nature and, on the other hand, those that can be understood only with reference also to other ideas. In Spinoza's terminology, in the first case, ideas are 'adequate'; in the second, they are 'inadequate'.

Spinoza's treatment of the distinction between 'adequacy' and 'inadequacy' involves carefully orchestrated, though sometimes perplexing, movements of thought. Following it involves shifting between the perspective of an individual mind as an idea within a totality of modes, and the consideration of that totality itself.

There is also an additional shift – towards the concept of God-or-substance, on which it all depends:

> When we say that God has this or that idea, not only insofar as he constitutes the nature of the human Mind, but in so far as he also has the idea of another thing together with the human Mind, then we say that the human Mind perceives the thing only partially, or inadequately. (EIIP11Cor.)

It may well seem a strange and cumbersome way of talking. Yet this diversion of talk about an individual mind through talk of God is fundamental to Spinoza's way of thinking of truth and error. The rerouting enacts, at the level of human thought, his metaphysics of substance, attributes and modes. A human mind's access to truth is construed through the interdependence of modes in a totality. That is the ontological basis of truth – and also the ontological basis of error.

What Spinoza describes as the 'inadequacy' of an idea is the other side of the coin to the interdependence of finite modes of substance, on which he insisted in *Ethics I*. He states the principle on which that inadequacy depends in a digression clarifying the nature of bodies, after EIIP13: 'All modes by which a body is affected by another body follow both from the nature of the body affected and at the same time from the nature of the affecting body . . .' (A1, following L3).

What goes for bodies, as finite modes of extension, goes also for finite modes of thought, which are ideas of body: 'The idea of any mode in which the human Body is affected by external bodies must involve the nature of the human Body and at the same time the nature of the external body' (EIIP16). It follows that 'The human Mind perceives the nature of a great many bodies together with the nature of its own body' (EIIP16Cor.1).

Putting all that together, a mind's knowledge of its own body – and hence of itself, as 'idea' of that body – is 'inadequate', rather than 'adequate'. Contrary to Descartes, human beings are, for Spinoza, not clear knowers of themselves. For a mind knows itself only through felt awareness of a body affected by other bodies.

What Spinoza calls 'inadequacy' haunts his treatment of the human mind's efforts to understand its own body, other bodies and itself. Descartes proposed criteria of truth, accessible to the mind's inspection of passive ideas within itself. In contrast, Spinoza's treatment of truth and error shifts focus to the positioning of active ideas within a totality – which includes itself. In this system, a mind's inclusion in the totality of Nature enters into the very nature of its knowing.

The role of imagination is crucial in this treatment of human knowing. It allows – indeed ensures – that the mind has available to it ideas of things that are no longer directly present to it. On Spinoza's account, the capacity to imagine reflects the complex structure of the human body, which allows retention of traces of its past affections by other bodies.

As I mentioned earlier, the details of that bodily complexity are sketched in the 'Digression on the Nature of Bodies', between Propositions 13 and 14 of *Ethics II*. Because human bodies are affected by other bodies – and are able to retain traces of those affections – a human mind is able to form the 'adequate' ideas through which reason comes to better understand the natures of things. However, that susceptibility of the human body to be affected by others is also the basis for a mind's having 'inadequate' ideas. By Spinoza's definitions, a mind's inadequate ideas involve the natures of other things, as well as the nature of its own body. Both inadequacy and adequacy in ideas are thus grounded in the interdependence of finite modes of extension.

All this amounts to a very different treatment of human knowing from that offered by Descartes. Spinoza's model involves taking seriously a mind's embodiment, and hence its being embedded in Nature. It also involves an upgrading of the role of imagination in human knowing. It is this shift that is the key to a Spinozist reconceptualising of human thought. To see its possible ramifications, we must now look in more detail at what becomes of the notions of truth, error and certainty in Spinoza's version of embodied knowing.

Adequacy, Inadequacy and 'Ideas of Ideas'

Spinoza's version of truth involves moving to the consideration of higher order ideas – those which have other ideas as their objects. This takes us to another level of his repudiation of Descartes's version of ideas as passive pictures, awaiting an external act of affirmation. Spinoza insists that the mind's inherent activity bypasses all need for criteria of certainty. Because ideas are themselves mental acts, to have 'ideas of ideas' comes, for him, to the same thing as knowing that one knows.

Talk of forming 'ideas of ideas' might suggest convoluted mental gymnastics. Yet for Spinoza this shift to another level of ideas is an obvious outcome of his treatment of the relation between mind and body as that of an idea to its object. 'The object of the idea constituting the human Mind is the Body, or a certain mode of Extension which actually exists, and nothing else' (*EIIP13*). A mind and its body are really one and the same, though they exist as different 'expressions' of the power of substance under different attributes.

In the context of his talk of higher level ideas, Spinoza reiterates the unity of mind and body, and reaffirms it as the principle of the unity between the idea of a mind and that mind itself: 'This idea of the Mind is united to the Mind in the same way as the Mind is united to the Body' (*EIIP21*). He adds that, just as a mind and its body are one and the same, so too 'the idea of the Mind and the Mind itself are one and the same thing' (*EIIP21Schol.*).

In a mind's relation to its body, the sameness holds across a difference in attributes. Mind and body are the same, though expressed under different attributes of substance. Mirroring the structure of that relation, the idea of the mind has that mind as its object. However, here the idea–object relation does not involve different attributes. It holds between different finite modes of substance, under the same attribute – thought.

In the same scholium to *EIIP21*, he goes on to connect that unity in difference to his forthcoming treatment of knowing that one knows: 'For as soon as someone knows something, he thereby knows that he knows it, and at the same time knows that he knows, and so on, to infinity'. Spinoza returns to the point, later in

Ethics II: 'He who has a true idea at the same time knows that he has a true idea, and cannot doubt the truth of the thing' (EIIP43). He goes on to elaborate it, adding in a scholium: 'For no one who has a true idea is unaware that a true idea involves the highest certainty. For to have a true idea means nothing other than knowing a thing perfectly, or in the best way' (EIIP43Schol.).

It may still seem a dogmatic assertion. However, Spinoza insists that if readers do not see this, it can only be because they persist in thinking of an idea as a mute thing, rather than as 'a mode of thinking, viz. the very [act of] understanding'. It is for him a consequence of seeing ideas as active that a mind knows that an idea agrees with its object simply by having the idea. There is a translucence here, in the relation between ideas and 'ideas of ideas', which Spinoza sees as bypassing any need for marks of truth. Truth, therefore, is for him 'its own standard' (EIIP43Schol.).

Spinoza's talk of an infinite series of 'knowing that one knows' may conjure up a giddying hall of mirrors. However, it is not meant to be a psychological exercise of consciously forming ideas of ideas, on to infinity. His point, I take it, is that – contrary to Descartes – there is no need for a contorted inspecting of ideas in the first place. The first supposed mental inspection and evaluation is for Spinoza no less absurd than the impossible completion of the ongoing acts of self-surveillance. To be certain is to 'know that we know'; and that certainty is already there in the first actual act of understanding. The focus, throughout, remains on the idea as of itself active, rather than passive.

Spinoza has shifted the challenge of authenticity from the properties of a passive mental picture to the performance of a mental act. Ideas are not passive items awaiting authentication by a freely acting will. Rather, they are self-authenticating acts of thinking. It might seem to a sceptic, though, that this shift involves a further sleight of hand. Spinoza has insisted that to have a true idea means nothing other than 'knowing a thing perfectly, or in the best way'. Yet might not the sceptic rejoin that there is still room for doubt about whether a mind does indeed, on any particular occasion, know 'in the best way'?

Spinoza is here considering ideas – as Descartes does in the *Meditations* – from a first-person perspective. There may be room for doubt about whether some mind other than one's own is engaging in its inner life 'in the best way'. However, Spinoza's point is that a mind cannot – while actively engaged in its own thinking – seriously entertain such a doubt. Within what he calls an idea – the occurrence of an act of thinking – he sees no room for doubt. For what he calls the object of the idea is not something external to – or separable from – the act itself. It is an internal determination of the content of the idea. It is thus the whole package – act and content together – that carries the assurance of truth as 'its own standard'.

The crucial point here is that, on the model Spinoza offers, truth is not to be construed as a dubitable correspondence between internal ideas and external things – any more than the mind itself is to be construed as externally related to the body as a separate entity. Neither in the one nor in the other case, can the act be prised apart from its object. There is a unity in difference here which mirrors, at the level of finite modes, that of attributes of the one substance.

What then is truth? Spinoza does not equate it with a defining mark of 'adequacy', possessed by some ideas and lacked by others. That would be to perpetuate the Cartesian model of truth as an identifiable property which the mind must discern in something presented to it. His formulation is subtly different. What is at stake is not a property, discernible in an idea. Rather, it is the manner in which an idea is present.

In clarification, Spinoza introduces a further distinction – addressed, not to the properties of ideas, but to the relations between them. 'The ideas of the affections of the human Body, *insofar as they are related only to the human Mind*, are not clear and distinct, but confused' (EIIP28, my emphasis). And later: 'Every idea that *in us* is absolute, or adequate and perfect, is true' (EIIP34, my emphasis).

The question then becomes: what exactly is it for an idea to be 'adequate in us'? The modifier 'in us' adds emphasis to the point that – in contrast to Descartes's 'clarity and distinctness' – Spinoza's 'adequacy' is not something that can be judged by consideration of that idea alone. What matters is how the idea is considered with regard to the totality of finite modes of which it is part.

On Spinoza's account, if an idea within a mind can be adequately understand without reference to other ideas – that is, without reference to ideas that are not included within the mind itself – then it can be said to be 'adequate in us'. In contrast, if it can be adequately understood only by taking into consideration some of those other ideas, then it is not 'adequate in us'. An idea is 'adequate in us' only when the mind in which it exists contains within itself all that is necessary to understand that idea.

Considered in the totality of finite modes of thought – in what Spinoza sometimes calls 'the mind of God' – there are no inadequate ideas. However, the ideas included in any one human mind form just a tiny grouping within that totality. The important point here was already implicit in Spinoza's earlier account of 'inadequacy':

> When we say that God has this or that idea, not only insofar as he constitutes the nature of the human Mind, but insofar as he also has the idea of another thing together with the human Mind, then we say that the human Mind perceives the thing only partially, or inadequately. (EIIP11Cor.)

In thus presenting human knowledge as a participation in 'the Mind of God' Spinoza has radically reconstrued human knowing as inherently immersed within 'the whole of Nature'. At the same time, he has reconstrued the internal relations of reason and imagination within a human mind. His emphasis on the wholeness of Nature is matched by an emphasis on the wholeness of the human mind.

Knowing Things, Oneself and God

What Spinoza calls 'common notions' – the ideas through which reason understands what things have in common – satisfy his description of being adequate 'in us'. Ideas of individual things – including the mind's idea of itself – do not. The idea of another mode involves not only the nature of the human body, but also 'at the same time the nature of the external body' (EIIP16). It follows that 'the human Mind perceives the nature of a great many bodies together with the nature of its own body' (EIIP16Cor.).

Spinoza has here offered a striking articulation of the human condition in relation to knowledge. On his account, in understanding the natures of things in accordance with the common notions of reason, a mind does not apprehend their individuality. And insofar as its understanding is directed to individuals, that understanding is unavoidably 'inadequate'. In Spinoza's treatment of knowledge, the apprehension of individuality requires the felt awareness of body, which is, for him, imagination. Hence, the singularity of things is not captured by ideas that are 'adequate in us'.

However, there is also another striking consequence of his treatment of reason's relations with imagination, which relates to the mind's awareness of itself. When a mind considers itself in relation to substance, the 'common notions' of reason can come together with the felt awareness of its own individual body. The mind's own continued existence – like that of other singular things – is mediated through the totality of finite modes. Yet it can have an unmediated understanding of its own relation to the power of substance, which maintains all things in existence. 'For even if each one is determined by another singular thing to exist in a certain way, still the force by which each one perseveres in existing follows from the eternal necessity of God's nature' (EIIP45Schol.).

A mind can thus have an immediate understanding of its own existence as a mode of substance, even though it does not fully understand all its inter-relations with ideas of other bodies. Spinoza's reflections on the status of an individual mind take him back to the theme of the interdependence of all finite modes. From considering itself in relation to substance, the mind is drawn to reflect anew on its own inclusion in the totality of Nature. There are significant ramifications for the mind's self-understanding.

It is helpful here to think of a human mind as positioned on two axes of dependence. Considered on the horizontal axis, it is interdependent with the totality of other finite modes. Considered on the vertical axis, its continued existence depends directly on substance, of which it is itself a mode. For Spinoza, those two ways of considering the continued existence of an individual mind do not cancel one another out. They are not in conflict; indeed, they are inter-related. A mind's own continued existence is mediated through that of other modes, which affect it and are affected by it. Yet it can grasp directly its own dependence on substance — its own status as a mode.

Here again, Spinoza's analysis of the status of a human mind differs starkly from that of the Cartesians he criticises. For Descartes the mind comes, through the exercise of methodical thinking, to a clear understanding of its own existence as a thinking individual substance — causally dependent on God its Creator, yet complete in its own being. For Spinoza, the mind, in coming to understanding itself as a mode of God-as-substance, is led to consider the mediation of its own continued existence through the totality of other finite modes. Hence, to understand its own status as a mode is to understand that it is but one amid the totality of other modes through which the being and power of substance is expressed, although its understanding of that totality is inevitably 'inadequate'.

Of course, Spinoza's talk of the mind understanding its own relation to God should not be construed on the model of a divine revelation from that God to human minds. There is no 'royal telephone' to a transcendent God from a supposedly sovereign kingdom within the whole of Nature. Yet Spinoza stresses that minds can come to understand themselves in direct relation to this version of God. That is, they can come to understand that they are indeed modes of substance. Here, what I have described as the 'vertical' and 'horizontal' axes of understanding a mind's dependence on substance come together. The mind comes to understand substance, of which it is a mode, as the basis for the existence of itself and of all the other finite modes, through which its own existence is nonetheless mediated.

Spinoza intimates to his readers that this realisation of a mind's status as a mode of substance is of great consequence for deep issues of life and of mortality, which they will see fully considered in *Ethics V*. In one of his most perplexing, yet intriguing pronouncements, Spinoza says that this self-understanding in relation to God is not to be construed in terms of duration. Rather, it is 'the very nature of existence, which is attributed to singular things because infinitely many things follow from the eternal necessity of God's nature in infinitely many modes'. It concerns 'the very existence of singular things insofar as they are in God' (EIIP45Schol.).

We will see more of Spinoza's thoughts on human mortality when he considers in *Ethics* V – the climax of the work – how a mind can come to understand itself 'under the form of eternity'. Meanwhile, towards the end of *Ethics* II, he elaborates another startling conclusion of his version of embodied knowing. The mind – immersed, as it is, in the totality of modes – has only inadequate understanding of itself. It nevertheless has an 'adequate and perfect' knowledge of God-or-substance, of which it is a mode. In the course of elaborating this claim, he makes some further important observations about how he construes imagination.

Spinoza argues that it is only because they confuse understanding with imagining that people believe they lack an 'adequate' idea of God-or-substance. Since imagination involves the felt awareness of other bodies acting on one's own, there is no possibility of imagining substance itself. Finding that impossible, the mind instead joins the name 'God' to images of familiar finite things it is accustomed to seeing.

On Spinoza's analysis, the mind's error here resides in not rightly applying names. It does not arise directly in active human thinking – in the having of ideas. Rather, it arises in interpersonal communication – in language. Spinoza illustrates his point by a comparison with a confusion that he regards as similar in kind, though no doubt less profound: an excited man who, in his confusion, reports that a neighbour's 'yard' has flown into his 'chicken'. The flaw does not reside in the man's own active thinking. It arises, rather, in the misuse of names through which his thought is communicated.

What content can be given to this 'adequate and perfect' knowledge of God? Spinoza claims the mind has it, despite its inability to adequately know the totality of finite modes. At this stage in the *Ethics*, he does not attempt to offer an explicit content for it – other than the definition of minds as modes of substance, enunciated in *Ethics* I. Rather, he attempts to wean the reader away from incredulity. He suggests that they cannot recognise their own understanding of God only because they look instead for an impossible imagining.

On Spinoza's line of thought here, despite the vehemence of religious controversies about the nature of God, the adequacy and perfection of human understanding of God is readily apparent. Putting all that together, his claim is that it seems to us that we lack adequate knowledge of God only because of those mistaken Cartesian assumptions about passive ideas and active free will, which he has rejected.

Imagination and Error

Spinoza's argumentation about the true nature of God has now returned to the issue of the right construal of error. He has completed a detour that began from his account, earlier in *Ethics II*, of the nature of imagining and its relations with error. He insisted there that imagination is not of itself a source of error. 'The Mind does not err from the fact that it imagines, but only in so far as it is considered to lack an idea that excludes the existence of those things it imagines to be present to it' (EIIP17Schol.). Error is thus grounded, not in misuse of a supposedly free will, but rather in the unavoidable fact that finite modes are continually affected by one another within a totality.

What emerges from all this is that, for Spinoza, imagination is not an enemy of the mind's access to truth; it enables, rather than impedes, it. We will see later that this is an important insight in relation to understanding and communicating the complex impacts of climate change. But it is important to first address Spinoza's strange talk of ideas excluding one another from existence and its bearing on how he sees the relations between imagination and reason.

Within the Cartesian model of error rejected by Spinoza, talk of 'excluding from existence' conjures up an act of will, in which a mind either accepts or rejects a passive mental object before it. Given that Spinoza rejects that model, what sense can he make of this process of exclusion? The clarification which he goes on immediately to offer is itself elusive:

> For, if the Mind, while it imagined non-existent things as present to it, at the same time knew that those things did not exist,

it would, of course, attribute this power of imagining to a virtue of its nature, not to a vice – especially if this faculty of imagining depended only on its own nature, i.e. (by ID7), if the Mind's faculty of imagining were free. (EP17Schol.)

By way of assistance to the reader, Spinoza thoughtfully provides at this point a reminder of his earlier definition of freedom:

> That thing is called free which exists from the necessity of its nature alone, and is determined to act by itself alone. But a thing is called necessary, or rather compelled, which is determined by another to exist and to produce an effect in a certain and determinate manner. (EID7)

The argument here may well be perplexing to contemporary readers. To clarify his claim that imagining is not of itself a source of error, Spinoza invites his readers to imagine something the existence of which he has himself denied – a 'free imagining'. However, the strategy becomes clearer if we keep in mind the two key features of his rejection of the Cartesian model of error – embodiment and interdependence.

Although the mind is the idea of its body, it knows that body only through the ways in which it is affected by other bodies: 'The human Mind does not know the human Body itself, nor does it know that it exists, except through ideas of affections by which the Body is affected' (EIIP19). An inherently embodied mind knows itself and other things only through felt changes in the body of which it is the idea; and that body is apprehended only through its interactions with other bodies. It is only through the bodily retention of past affections that a mind can think of what is not currently affecting its body. Hence the crucial importance of imagination to human thought and knowledge.

Spinoza entertains the fiction that human imagining is 'free' in order to bring out more forcefully the nature of imagination and its role in human knowing. Human imagination cannot summon up before itself something that bears no relation to past experience. A 'free' imagining, in contrast, would be able to apprehend things regardless of the limitations of bodily experience. The important upshot of the intellectual exercise here is that a 'free' imagining would not be – as human imagination is – embodied.

It is a confusing argument, and perhaps not entirely a strategic success. What does become clear, nonetheless, is that Spinoza regards imagination as a positive feature of a human mind. The capacity to have before it what no longer exists is neither a weakness nor an aberration.

Here the full significance of the contrast between Spinoza's approach to error and that of Descartes becomes apparent. The existence of error is for Spinoza an inevitable consequence of the human mind's embodiment, which involves its interconnection with other finite modes. Proneness to error is grounded in the very nature of an embodied mind; it is a susceptibility due neither to a natural defect nor to an aberration. It reflects in thought the remarkable capacity of the human body to retain traces of ways in which it has in the past been affected by other finite bodily modes. To be prone to 'inadequate' understanding is thus an inevitable consequence of a human mind's being the idea of one body among others.

Reason and Freedom

All this has consequences for the status of human reason. As we have seen, the bodily complexity that makes error possible – the capacity to retain traces of past affections – is also a precondition of the capacity to form the 'common notions' of reason, through which a mind comes to understand what different ideas have in common. Proneness to error and the capacity for reasoning are thus both framed by a human mind's inclusion in the totality of being.

For Spinoza, a human mind is a conglomerate of adequate and inadequate ideas. It encompasses, along with ideas of its present affections, the reverberations of earlier ones. Within this conglomerate of past and present affections, the mind strives, through the exercise of reasoning, to come to better understanding of itself, of God and of the rest of the world.

In this model of human knowing, reason retains a distinctive power that provides the basis for a new version of freedom. Through forming 'ideas of ideas', the mind is able to form sequences of ideas which are not bound by the fortuitous succession of impacts of other bodies on its own. Spinoza talks in this context of a contrast between the 'order of reason' and 'the common order of nature'.

A mind's understanding of things is inadequate or confused, Spinoza says, 'so long as it perceives things from the common order of nature', determined by 'fortuitous encounters with things' (EIIP29Schol.). In contrast, there is 'the order of reason', in which ideas are organised differently from the sequence in which they happen to arise in a particular mind. The 'order of reason' accords with the freedom of the mind – as that is articulated in Spinoza's definition of freedom at EID7. It depends only on what the mind finds within itself – on what can be grasped through its understanding of its own 'adequate' ideas.

In the later parts of the *Ethics*, Spinoza will elaborate the power – and the limitations – of that freedom of the human mind within the 'common order of Nature'. As we will see, this power is exerted within the necessities of the whole of Nature, rather than through a privileged exemption from those necessities. For Spinoza, freedom coexists with necessity; and the mind's access to truth is haunted by the ever-present possibility of error.

Spinoza's description of the actual occurrence of error evokes a dynamic struggle among ideas. That struggle mirrors – under the attribute of thought – the struggle to persist in existence that goes on between bodily modes. At the heart of error there is lack or absence; but what is lacked is not an exercise of free will. What Spinoza talks of as a lack of 'exclusion' of one idea by others involves the lingering of a past affection, which is not overcome by the power of others occurring in the present.

The activity involved in that 'excluding' comes from ideas themselves – construed as mental acts. In the concluding sections of *Ethics II*, Spinoza reiterates this emphasis on the inherent activity of ideas. 'In the Mind there is no volition, or affirmation and negation, except that which the idea involves insofar as it is an idea' (EIIP49). The 'exclusion' does not happen through the exercise of human will. Rather, the activity inherent in the one idea is, as it were, overpowered by the stronger force of others.

Increasingly, the language in which Spinoza describes error evokes a mental analogue of motion and rest, and of competing forces for existing. Error resides, not in an act of will exerted in the present, but in the absence of a countervailing present idea, whose greater force could prevail against one that lingers from a past affection. Spinoza goes on to make more explicit just how this dynamic treatment of ideas transforms the understanding of doubt and certainty:

> A false idea, insofar as it is false, does not involve certainty. When we say that a man rests in false ideas, and does not doubt them, we do not, on that account, say that he is certain, but only that he does not doubt, or that he rests in false ideas because there are no causes to bring it about that his imagination wavers. (EIIP49Schol.1)

The crucial point here is that for Spinoza certainty resides in the mental activity inherent in ideas themselves – in the act of thinking, which leaves no room for doubt. A mind not adequately performing those acts of thinking 'rests' in falsity. Such a mind has not yet been made to vacillate or waver. It is striking that, on this analysis, a mind's 'wavering' has become, as it were, the portal to the more powerful mental activity which is of itself the assurance of truth.

The Trajectory of the *Ethics*

Spinoza's argumentation has moved a long way here. Its trajectory began with a disagreement with the Cartesians about the epistemology of error. It then proceeded to consider the immersion of a human mind in the totality of being. That yielded the initially startling affirmation of a human mind's inclusion in the divine nature. Finally, the discussion returns to the nature of error – now explicated through his version of the 'exclusion' of ideas by one another.

That movement of thought maps the journey Spinoza wanted his readers to enact. From the metaphysics of thought and matter in *Ethics I*, they are led to consider, in *Ethics II*, the nature of human knowing. The reader is left at that point with an intimation of the deep issues of human life and mortality, to be considered more fully in *Ethics V*. Between the treatment of error in *Ethics II* and that fuller treatment of its upshot in *Ethics V* lies the treatment, in *Ethics III* and *Ethics IV*, of the nature of human emotions and their role in the good life, which forms an important part of the whole story.

For contemporary readers of Spinoza, there will be much that seems strange in his treatment of knowledge, truth and error. From a Spinozist perspective, that might just indicate that human minds remain, in current times, in the thrall of a Cartesian model of the life of the mind. For Spinoza that model is an obstacle – not just to understanding human knowing, but also to living a good human life. Living well, he argues, demands understanding that human minds are inherently embodied, and hence fully immersed in the totality of interdependent finite things.

On Spinoza's model, human minds remain distinctive within the totality of finite modes – as ideas of human bodies. Yet those bodies are themselves not insulated from other bodily forces. Better understanding those interconnections within wholeness might, in present times, enable a more nuanced treatment of mind and thought – better attuned to understanding the vicissitudes of human lives amid planetary change.

Even if contemporary readers cannot go all the way with Spinoza, trying to make some sense of these insights can open up possibilities for rethinking, in their own terms, the relations between human and non-human within a shared totality. Rather than unreflectively anthropomorphising the non-human, it might then become possible to develop an expanded and enriched understanding of mind and thought, encompassing human and non-human in broader unities.

At a time when the accelerating impacts of climate change are accompanied by rapid growth in the achievements of artificial intelligence, Spinoza's insights might also facilitate a revaluation of what is distinctive – and irreplaceable – in human thinking. In *Ethics III*, Spinoza further clarifies his treatment of the wholeness of human minds, showing how emotion, as well as imagination, is structurally integrated with reason.

3

The Whole Mind

In the history of Western thought, human beings have long occupied a somewhat ambiguous and ambivalent position in the world – in aspiration, perhaps, like gods, yet all too earthly in the limitations and vulnerabilities of their lives. The possession of reason has been the pivot of that tension. It has been seen as the distinguishing mark that separates humanity from the rest of Nature. Yet its own separation from lesser aspects of being human is complex and contested.

Unease in the sense of human superiority in Nature has its correlate in reason's uneasy relationships with other aspects of mental life, which make would-be gods unavoidably human. I have argued that Spinoza's insistence that human minds do not transcend what later came to be called 'nature without' involves a radical challenge also to familiar, but troubled, assumptions about the status of reason in 'nature within'. There are human situations that demand rational understanding, yet also challenge the resources of intellect acting alone.

In *Ethics III* Spinoza continues his treatment of reason, now addressing its inter-relations with emotion as well as with imagination. The integrative model that emerges bears, in interesting ways, on some of the complexities of current concern with climate change emotion.

Climate Change Emotion

The human experience of time is a focal point for the sense of disruption of what is familiar, under the experience of climate change. There is, for a start, its impact on the sense of human finitude. Awareness of mortality has itself undergone change throughout human history. Yet, in the past, it has been possible for a sense of individual human life – contingent though its span is – to be framed by expectation of continuing human presence in the world, reaching into an indefinite future.

Apocalyptic climate change scenarios have tended to focus on the impending demise of human civilisation, rather than on the possible extinction of the human species. Yet even the less extreme scenarios of a dramatically changed human future can unsettle the familiar, untroubled sense of temporal passage.

The assumption of continuity of the human species – especially when bolstered by an expectation of ever-increasing 'growth' or 'progress' – can provide a measure of reassurance in the face of individual mortality. Intimation of a future in which one does not oneself exist, yet others will do so, may be experienced as sadness at impending loss of what they will continue to enjoy. Yet it may also yield solace in the thought that what matters most in one's own life will continue through the concerns and efforts of others. In the lack of that familiar sense of assured human futurity, the unease of individual finitude is intensified.

The future is commonly conceptualised as a realm of uncertainty: what will happen is not yet determined. Yet, in a familiar collective mindset, the future is not construed as a realm of mere hope. There is a common expectation that the lives of future generations will be better – or at least not worse – than what has gone before.

Narratives of perfectibility and progress underlie much contemporary rhetoric of optimism in the face of the future. They are often reinforced by metaphors of resistance, endurance and ultimate victory. Such rhetoric can feed the denial or minimising of climate change, allowing its manifest effects to be construed as glitches in an ongoing story of triumphal progress, in which humanity fights back against external threats. Hope is then recast as assurance of deliverance, grounded in human transcendence of Nature – a confident affirmation of future well-being, whatever the grief or trauma along the way.

In addition to shaking the expectation of indefinite progress, the emotional impact of climate change can bring also a less direct, though deeper, unsettling of the very sense of futurity that frames and sustains the vicissitudes of individual lives. There can be radical uncertainty, even in judging just how future those impacts may be. They may hover in consciousness as a vaguely articulated fear at what might happen at an indeterminate time. Yet, as collective understanding becomes better informed by the mounting evidence, the gap between ominous futurity and present reality is ever narrowing.

There is disparity in the apprehended pace of change. For some, climate change looms as an imminent apocalyptic end of all that is familiar. For others, it continues to be seen as a long-term process, allowing some scope either for mitigation or for adaptation. Either way, awareness of climate change destabilises the sense of the future.

A shifting sense of the past is also at play in emotional response to climate change. In a rich analysis, the Australian geographer Lesley Head has commented on ways in which notions of an idealised pristine past – from which effects of human presence have been erased – can shape a flawed attitude towards such concepts as conservation. Idealised past conditions then become a baseline for actions of restoration. 'Against such an ideal, the present can hardly be understood in any other terms than loss.'[1] The idealising of a lost past in common narratives around climate change can reinforce a sense of the future as 'an unimaginable time-space of potential catastrophe'.[2]

In finding space for hope in the midst of informed awareness of climate change, Head argues against the conflation of hope with optimism; and for a rethinking of its assumed status as a subjective emotional disposition. In the context of response to climate change, she suggests, hope can find expression 'as practice, as keeping on going'. 'Hope is practised and performed; it is a sort of hybrid, vernacular collective worked out in everyday practice and experience.'[3]

[1] Head 2016: 41.
[2] Ibid. 49.
[3] Ibid. 90.

Thus construed, hope is different from a subjective state of confidence in assured outcomes. It can be incentivised, rather than overwhelmed, by grief at species loss and damage.

The Distinction Between Hope and Optimism

The appeal of a contrast between hope and optimism can be reinforced by noting here a comparable distinction that was drawn, in the eighteenth century, in Voltaire's powerful articulation of the inherent direction of hope towards the future. The philosophical context was Voltaire's provocative challenge to a mentality of metaphysically based optimism – belief in the actuality of the 'best of all possible worlds'. He attributed that belief – not entirely fairly – to Leibniz, among others.

Voltaire was outraged that a philosophical doctrine could claim that the actual world is the best possible. His scorn was directed, not least, to what he saw as the implications for hope. He saw metaphysical optimism as endorsing a cruel philosophy, under a consoling description – not so much an affirmation of hope, as one which drives to despair those who embrace it. Voltaire's central point was trenchantly expressed in his poem on an eighteenth-century challenge to habitual expectations – the disastrous Lisbon earthquake of 1757. Responding to those he saw as metaphysical optimists, he wrote, in his 'Poem on the Lisbon Disaster', that while thinking that all will be well is an expression of hope, the belief that all now is well is an illusion.

Voltaire's point was that true hope demands an orientation towards a future imagined as better than the present. Thus construed, hope finds expression in a determination to make the actual world better. He saw practical response to human suffering – whether produced by natural disasters or by political injustice – as undermined by the doctrine that things are really 'all well' now.

Hope – thus seen as inherently directly towards the future – was for Voltaire an expression of what it is to be human. At the end of his Lisbon poem, he suggests that an all-powerful being would, in its might and immensity, lack the common afflictions of human life – evil, ignorance, distress and sin. Yet, he observes, such a being would also lack one thing more: hope. He saw hope as a reflection – and expression – of lack of power. Yet, in its orientation towards an imagined better future, it carries the seeds of transformation of human presence in the world. Thus Voltaire offered a way of thinking of hope that distinguished it from what he saw as a facile optimism.

Voltaire went on to create, in the character of Pangloss in *Candide*, a satirical parody of what he saw as grotesque in the metaphysical optimism that turned hope into an affirmation that all is really 'all well' now. *Candide* is an unfair representation of the philosophical import of Leibniz's doctrine that the actual world is the best possible – a doctrine which was itself, among other things, a repudiation of Spinoza's denial of divine free will. The God of Leibniz's *Theodicy* chooses – among an infinite range of interconnected possibles – a world rationally judged to be the best overall. However, Leibniz did not claim – as Voltaire seems to have suggested he did – that what was chosen by God was, whether his creatures knew it or not, the best possible arrangement of the totality of Creation to ensure ultimate human well-being.

Leibniz's 'best possible' world combined the most possibilities without falling into contradiction. That did not mean that everything that happens within it is good for human beings. Voltaire wrongly targeted Leibniz. Yet his separation of hope from optimism remains an important insight, which can illuminate the emotional repercussions of the sense of a fragile human future, under conditions of climate change.

Unlike Leibniz, Spinoza rejected the whole idea of a purposefully designed world, and the associated need for an explanation or justification of things being as they are. In that respect, the spirit of his philosophy has more in common with Voltaire than with Leibniz. Read now, Spinoza's philosophy can yield significant insights into how it is possible for hope to persist, where optimism fades.

Insights from *Ethics III* may also help make sense of another striking juxtaposition in some climate change writing: the interconnections between hope and grief. Strange though that concatenation may initially seem, hope and grief can be seen to take on a new configuration in the context of the destabilising of temporal consciousness in the context of climate change.

Climate Change Grief and the Phenomenology of Time

Contemporary understanding of human presence in the world carries a residue of past imaginings. That residue becomes visible in the emotional impact of realising how the world is changing under human presence, and how human self-awareness is itself changing. Often, that realisation is imbued with a strong sense of loss – a kind of grief, which involves both the sense of place and that of time. It is as if the conceptual construct of the world as an amalgam of the 'natural' and the 'human' comes into clearer view in the very perception of its shattering.

Such disorientation can be particularly intense when awareness of the ongoing transformation of old landforms, under human presence, comes together with a sense of the inevitability of future loss. Reflecting – in an anthology of essays on climate change emotion – on Australian landscapes lost under European settlement, the novelist James Bradley comments on the destruction awaiting those same terrains under unstoppable sea-level rise:

> And so, just as this landscape bears within itself the memory of other, far older landscapes, it also contains this future landscape. In this it illustrates the way in which climate change deranges temporality, collapsing geological and human time into each other, and freighting not just the past, but also this now-unavoidable future with grief and loss.[4]

The sudden onset of grief is often articulated by those directly experiencing the impacts of climate change; the emotional response can be inseparable from the intellectual realisation. Writing of Australia's catastrophic bushfires of 2019–20, the editors of that same volume talk of the immediacy of a sense of loss – not only of fellow humans, but of incomprehensible numbers of animals, insects, fungi and forests: 'All kin, all gone'. In that context, talk of kinship becomes something more than mere metaphor. Out of the sense of loss comes intensified insight into the truth of

---

[4] Bradley 2020a: 234–5.

interconnection.⁵ An earlier volume, which brings together interdisciplinary scholars, artists and writers under the title *Arts of Living on a Damaged Planet*, also explores the theme of 'ghosts' of lost pasts, futures lost to mass extinctions, and the haunting of present landscapes by the imagined dire futures that might come to replace them.⁶

Hope and grief may seem unlikely companions. Yet the possibility of a shared symbolism uniting them has been recognised in literary expression, and in contemporary philosophical reflection. The American poet Emily Dickinson famously gave poetic expression to hope as the warm, gentle feathered thing, perched in the afflicted soul. Yet things with feathers can also have powerful associations with dread. In his poetic novella *Grief Is the Thing with Feathers*, the British author Max Porter has structured an iconography of grief around a fictional giant crow, which makes a noisy entry into the home of a bereaved family, with a smothering smell of decaying plumage.

In the bereaved household which is the setting of Porter's novella, two troubled children are confronted with musty black feathers, which have not come from the comforting soft down of their pillows, while their grieving father withdraws into the embrace of the monstrous bird. What follows is a poignant and powerful exploration of the poetics of grief. 'Crow' has come to stay, insisting that he won't leave until he knows he is no longer needed.⁷

Porter's evocation of disrupted temporality in prolonged grieving is subjected to a more directly philosophical treatment in his Introduction to an essay on grief by the British poet and philosopher Denise Riley. Part memoir, part philosophical essay, her *Time Lived, Without Its Flow* explores the impact of grief on temporal consciousness – its little analysed, yet commonly experienced disruption of the 'flow' of time.⁸ Central to Riley's analysis is the insight that the normal sense of futurity involves an ongoing

---

⁵ Muir et al. 2020: 12–13.
⁶ Tsing et al. 2017.
⁷ Porter 2015: 7
⁸ Riley 2019.

sense of movement. The fragility of that accustomed orientation towards the future becomes visible in the experience of confinement to the present, in the sudden onset of grief.

There are resonances here, as Riley notes in passing, of ancient Stoic talk of detachment from concern with the future. For Seneca, what connected hope with fear was the tendency to be fretted by a sense of the future, rather than being focused on the present. In Riley's account, in contrast, loss of concern with the future is an aberration, which does not yield a positive form of living in the present. Yet, it brings enhanced awareness of the pervasive sense of futurity that had previously been there, unnoticed.

Riley's exacting philosophical analysis reinforces the distinction between hope and optimism. What goes missing in the onset of grief is not an external basis for hope – a reason to look to the future. It is something more fundamental. It may seem that, if hope involves orientation towards the future, the experience of losing that orientation must be one of despair. Yet what emerges here is not a picture of pathological hopelessness, but rather a deep insight into the normal experience of 'temporal flow'.

Riley talks of that loss of 'flow' as resting on a 'transfer of affect' between living and dead – as if those in deep grief enter on the futureless being of the one mourned. It is as if they take on, in their own emotion, the dead one's loss of futurity.[9] What is at stake here is not some mystical or ineffable experience granted to the grieving. Nor is it presented as a condition of pathological obsession, to be therapeutically resolved. It is a point about the interplay of deep emotion and the human experience of time.

Riley's reflections on that interplay are primarily concerned with individual grief. However, there are insights here that are helpful for better understanding also the collective aspects of grief, which can be fruitfully explored in the context of climate change.

There is much that is unclear in the very notion of 'collective grief'. When well-meaning sympathisers claim to 'share' a person's grief – or even to know how it feels – the appropriate response may be polite incredulity. Authentic collective grief is most clearly understood in what is perhaps its most basic form – the directly

[9] Ibid. 45–6.

shared experience of loss. It is manifest in images of those stunned by the immediate experience of mass calamities – whether their form be 'natural', human-induced or ambiguously hybrid. It is common for such disasters to evoke expressions of grief, from those not directly affected: 'The whole nation grieves with you' is a common political mantra. Yet, welcome though the empathetic concern of others may be, the suggestion that a whole nation experiences the grief may well seem hollow.

Riley's talk of a 'transfer of affect' is more nuanced than common talk of 'sharing' grief. She discusses briefly the interesting possibility that this aspect of grief – reaching beyond the borders of individual selfhood – can yield an 'enlargement of human sympathy' through successive generations.[10] Although she is not talking of responses to climate change, it is an insight that bears on some of the complexities in climate change grief.

If grief can shake the normal sense of orientation towards the future, perhaps there is an analogous shared loss in the context of climate change. What is lost here is the sense of forward movement of humanity into a collective future. It is a feeling of loss on behalf of the species as a whole – present and past, living and dead; and perhaps even, beyond that, an empathetic 'transfer of affect' to other species.

What Riley calls 'transfer of affect' appears, paradoxically, to cross the insuperable divide between living and dead, which is at the core of grief. Her brief discussion illuminates not only the normal sense of temporal flow, but also the interconnections – the 'enlargement of sympathy' – which can bind human beings to one another across generations. Perhaps, under the emotional impacts of climate change, that enlargement can also extend to non-human parts of Nature.

Against the background of contemporary reflections on climate change emotion, I want now to turn to *Ethics III* and *IV*, to explore how Spinoza's treatment of reason, imagination and emotion, in the wholeness of a human mind, might fruitfully be brought to bear on these issues.

---

[10] Ibid. 22.

Reason: Supremacy or Integration?

Throughout his general treatment of emotion in *Ethics III* – and also in his further consideration of specific emotions in *Ethics IV* – Spinoza returns to his account of error, elaborating and refining it to show how it bears on the inter-relations of reason, imagination and emotion. On his account, all three are involved in a human mind's ongoing struggle for adequate understanding, and for continued well-being.

Central to Spinoza's treatment of emotion is his previous claim that vacillations within the mind are enmeshed with – though not caused by – bodily struggles to persist in being. In *Ethics II*, in the 'Digression on the Nature of Bodies', between Propositions 13 and 14, he explained that the preservation of an individual body involves its component parts keeping 'the same ratio of motion and rest to each other as before' (EIIP13A2L3). That now becomes the basis for his analysis of the affects.

It is interesting to note here that Spinoza uses the same Latin term *ratio* to cover both the notion of proportion and that of reason as intellectual process.[11] His double use of the term *ratio* is not incidental to Spinoza's treatment, in *Ethics III* and *IV*, of the inter-relations between the strivings to persist of individual minds and bodies. Bodily conatus, as the persistence of a proportion of motion and rest, has its correlate in the mind's efforts to better understand the nature of its own body in relation to others.

Spinoza's treatment of emotion echoes, and at times directly parallels, what he has previously said about imagination. His definitions and demonstrations in *Ethics II* connected imagination with the efforts of an embodied mind to understand – and with the possibility of error inherent in those efforts. In *Ethics III* and *IV*, he connects also emotions – affects – with those unstable efforts to understand.

Spinoza defines affects in terms of a mind's transitions between activity and passivity. Hence, by his previous definitions, they are conceptually connected with fluctuations in adequacy of

---

[11] For an interesting collection of essays exploring the ramifications of Spinoza's multiple uses of 'ratio', see Lord 2018.

understanding. Early in *Ethics III*, he observes that 'the Mind is more liable to passions the more it has inadequate ideas, and conversely, is more active the more it has adequate ideas' (EIIIP1Cor.).

Those connections of the affects with adequacy and inadequacy in ideas involve subtle variations in activity and passivity. There can be adequate ideas of transition to lesser activity, as well as inadequate ideas of increases in activity. At the centre of the analysis is Spinoza's identification of joy, sadness and desire as the basic transitions in mental activity, through which all the other emotions can be defined.

Affects can be negative passions, associated with the passivity of inadequate understanding. However, there are also positive affects, which are related to the mind insofar as it acts. For Spinoza a mind's coming to better understand the passions that impede its activity is key to remedying their destructive effects. Yet this remedy does not involve losing the mental enrichment of affectivity. Such transitions from passion to active emotion, through understanding, is not the work of reason alone. Its power over the passions depends on an alliance with operations of the imagination, forged through experience: 'The Mind, as far as it can, strives to imagine those things that increase or aid the Body's power of acting' (EIIIP12).

Such, for Spinoza, are the consequences of humanity's being immersed in Nature, rather than standing above it. He will sum the situation up, early in *Ethics IV*: 'We are acted on, insofar as we are a part of Nature, which cannot be conceived through itself, without the others' (EIVP2). The picture that emerges is that the continued existence of a human mind involves a confused confluence of mental processes, in which reason must interact and collaborate with – rather than suppress – imagination and emotion. At the core of that interaction is the mind's striving for better understanding of its own presence within the totality of things.

Throughout *Ethics III* and *IV*, Spinoza elaborates those interactions of reason, imagination and emotion. Much of what he has to say about the well-lived human life accords with the high estimation of reason common in the history of Western philosophy.

Yet his account of its integration with imagination and emotion makes for a very different way of thinking of the nature and scope of reason.

Spinoza's affirmation of reason is subtly nuanced. Rather than being treated as transcending mere Nature, it remains a vulnerable power within it. Its interdependence with imagination and emotion reflects a human mind's own limited position within the totality of things. In that respect, Spinoza's account of a unified human mind differs in important ways from the celebrated supremacy of reason, often associated with 'rationalism'. Yet reason retains here its crucial role in human thriving.

The Preface to *Ethics III* is a striking demonstration of the anomalies in categorising Spinoza as a 'rationalist'. It opens with a resounding affirmation of his rejection of the Cartesian model of the mind. Spinoza acknowledges that Descartes, in his *Passions of the Soul*, had investigated – with deductive rigour and insight – the nature of human passions, and the positive role they can play in the good life – along with the need to remedy their destructive effects. Yet he argues that the way Descartes went about that investigation was itself a manifestation of the basic flaw in his treatment of human knowing.

Spinoza asserts in the Preface that Descartes – despite 'the acuity of his observations' – did not break free of the deep error of treating human affects as 'outside nature'. The Cartesian figuration of human beings had them somehow disturbing, rather than following, the 'order of nature'. Again, Spinoza relates that error to the role assigned to human free will in attaining knowledge – to the belief that human beings have in principle 'absolute power' over their actions; that they are 'determined' by nothing other than themselves.

The complexity of Spinoza's attitude towards reason is visible in this Preface. In outlining how he will proceed in his treatment of affects, he says that he will subject them to the kind of study which takes seriously the fact that they occur in accordance with 'the universal laws of nature', which are 'always and everywhere the same'. He will treat the nature and powers of the affects, and the power of the mind over them, by the same method he has used previously in treating God and the mind: 'I shall consider human actions and appetites just as if it were a Question of lines, planes and bodies' (EIIIPreface).

In stating his intentions to pursue the study of human emotions in that way, Spinoza projects a philosophical persona that does, in some ways, fit with the retrospective construct of a 'rationalist' epistemology. He affirms the notion of an order of Nature, accessed by rational investigation. The geometric style introduced in his metaphysics of substance, attributes and modes in *Ethics I* – and extended to the consideration of human minds and bodies in *Ethics II* – is now to be sustained in *Ethics III*, though he is now concerned with the apparently messier subject matter of human desires and passions. Yet, despite that enactment of rational order in its form, the content of *Ethics III* offers a much more nuanced treatment of the inter-relations of reason, imagination and emotion than might be expected from the associations of later 'rationalism'.

Even in its exercise in theoretical inquiry, human reason is for Spinoza framed by the inescapable embodiment of human minds within the whole of Nature. Throughout *Ethics III*, the power of reason in inquiry into the natures of things – including study of the irrationalities of human lives – is held in tension with its integration with imagination and emotion, in a broader concern with human well-being. Imagination – with its vacillations or fluctuations – was at the heart of Spinoza's treatment of the nature of human knowing in *Ethics II*. Those fluctuations now figure also in his treatment of the affects – along with echoes of his earlier talk of relations of 'exclusion' between ideas.

Indeed, at times, the relation, on the one hand, between emotional vacillation and, on the other, the role of the imagination in doubt, goes beyond a mere parallelism. The mind's vacillation between contrary affects, he says, is 'related to the affect as doubt is to the imagination; nor do vacillations of mind and doubt differ from one another, except in degree'. Both in relation to knowledge and in relation to emotion, vacillation arises from the fact that the human body is composed of 'a great many individuals of different natures' and so 'can be affected in a great many ways by one and the same body'. Within that constant change, one and the same object can be the cause of 'many and contrary affects' (EIIIP17Schol.).

For Spinoza, human knowledge and human emotion alike reflect the inter-relations of the human body within the totality of finite modes. Imagination, as the felt awareness of those fluctuations, is integrated into the exercise of reason – both in understanding the nature of the affects, and in managing their vagaries effectively, in order to know how best to live.

Activity and Passivity: The Classification of Emotions

The canvas on which Spinoza sketches the complex inter-relations of emotions has already been prepared by his earlier treatment in *Ethics II* of dynamic strivings – articulated through the notion of conatus, and its connections with the actual essences of finite modes. That conceptual apparatus – already linked with his definitions of 'adequate' and 'inadequate' ideas – now becomes the basis for a distinction between active and passive affects. Describing the passive affects – passions – he says that they 'are not related to the Mind except insofar as it has something which involves a negation, or insofar as it is considered as a part of nature which cannot be perceived clearly and distinctly through itself, without the others' (EIIIP3Schol.).

Here again, the embodied existence of a mind, and its insertion into a totality of finite modes, are two sides of the one coin. Fluctuation in bodily powers in relation to one another underlie – in a noncausal relation – the inter-relations and interactions of the affects. Against the background of those principles, previously enunciated in repudiating the Cartesian model of knowledge, Spinoza goes on to now offer his treatment of specific affects and their role in enhancing or impeding the good human life.

What Spinoza offers is not an exhaustive account of specific human emotions. There are, he says, as many species of each affect 'as there are species of objects by which we are affected' (EIIIP56). He considers it not necessary that he deal with all of them, for his purpose is only to determine their powers and the power of the mind over them (EIIIP56Schol.).

It is nonetheless striking that the 'active affects' that Spinoza selects for special attention are those that seem most readily associated with the role traditionally given to reason in philosophical accounts of the well-lived life – those which are related to the mind's power of understanding. However, the role he gives reason is very differently construed from a more familiar emphasis on its dominance over emotion.

Despite his insistence on the unity of mind and body, Spinoza's analysis allows for affects to be considered 'in relation to the Mind', prescinding from their bodily correlates. Yet his resort to a recurring locution of 'insofar as' makes it clear that he is here consciously prescinding from the full reality of an integrated structure, rather than affirming a supremacy of reason over other elements in the structure. In some cases he also introduces a further prescinding – narrowing his focus to the consideration of affects in relation to the mind 'insofar as it understands'.

That narrowing of focus allows Spinoza to classify affects with reference to their respective relations to what reason 'dictates'. Thus he can distinguish tenacity from nobility. Tenacity is: 'the Desire by which each one strives, solely from the dictate of reason, to preserve his being'. Nobility is 'the Desire by which each one strives, solely from the dictate of reason, to aid other men and join them to him in friendship' (EIIIP59Schol.).

Spinoza's descriptions of character traits – though their names may be unusual – evoke more familiar notions of the role of reason in the good life, which celebrate its cultivation in preference to emotion. Yet the guiding thought underlying his reference to 'dictates of reason' is very different. According to Spinoza, it is only insofar as reason can itself be affective that it has power in relation to the affects. Thus, the strength of tenacity and nobility is described in terms of their relations to desire, which is itself an affect. All this gives a distinctive twist to Spinoza's treatment of the place of reason, in general, in relation to the management of the affects.

The principles behind Spinoza's selection of particular affects for attention is not always obvious; and there is room for disagreement about the details of his treatment of them. From a contemporary perspective, what he sees as salient in his classification of emotions is often quaintly of his time – and not always charmingly so. There is, for example, his analysis of jealousy as 'a vacillation of mind born of Love and Hatred together, accompanied by the idea of another who is envied'. Elaborating, he gives prominence to the situation of the jealous man who is forced to 'join the image of the thing he loves to the image of him he hates'. This predicament, he explains, is found for the most part in 'Love toward a woman':

> For he who imagines that a woman he loves prostitutes herself to another not only will be saddened, because his own appetite is restrained, but also will be repelled by her, because he is forced to join the image of the thing he loves to the shameful parts and excretions of the other. (EIIIP 35Schol.)

What is most important for my purposes here is not the often dubious nuances of Spinoza's descriptions of specific emotions, which can be seen as reflecting social attitudes of his time. What is significant is his recurring contrast between steadiness and vacillation, which runs in tandem with the active/passive distinction – as a broad indicator of the division between positive and more negative emotions. The theme of mental fluctuation or vacillation is always there, reflecting Spinoza's constant insistence on the embodiment of the human mind, and its inclusion in the totality of finite modes.

In summing up what he takes himself to have shown in his general discussion of emotion, Spinoza is willing to use the term 'affect' interchangeably with 'vacillation':

> I have explained and shown . . . the main affects and vacillations of mind which arise from . . . Desire, Joy and Sadness. From what has been said it is clear that we are driven about in many ways by external causes, and that, like waves on the sea, driven by contrary winds, we toss about, not knowing our outcome and fate. (EIIIP59Schol.)

As a lament on the vicissitudes of human life, that metaphor of waves and contrary winds could have been used by any one of many ancient writers. However, Spinoza has given an old theme new content by articulating human vulnerability through a vivid reconceptualising of the location of human reason within the world. The sense of being tossed by contrary forces is accentuated by his emphasis on the infinite range of impacts on a human body, reflected in the inevitable fluctuations among a mind's ideas.

Spinoza's treatment of the affects emphasises the human body's extreme susceptibility to being affected by bodies external to it. 'Different men can be affected differently by one and the same object; and one and the same man can be affected differently at different times by one and the same object' (EIIIP51). So it can happen that 'what the one loves, the other hates, what the one fears, the other does not, and that one and the same man may now love what before he hated, and now dare what before he was too timid for' (EIIIP51Schol.).

An important aspect of Spinoza's emphasis on the dynamic fluctuations of mental life is the reversal of common ways of thinking of good and evil, in relation to human desire. In discussing that relation Spinoza says that by 'good' he understands:

> every kind of Joy, and whatever leads to it, and especially what satisfies any kind of longing, whatever that may be . . . For . . . we desire nothing because we judge it to be good, but on the contrary, we call it good because we desire it . . . So each one, from his own affect, judges, or evaluates, what is good and what is bad . . . (EIIIP39Schol.)

From the perspective of contemporary readers, that might sound like a 'relativist' dismissal of the objectivity of reason in relation to ethical judgement. In Spinoza's own times, his reversal of the relations between desire and 'good' fed common perceptions of him as an amoral atheist. However, for Spinoza, that reversal does not undermine the possibility of objective judgement. It reconstrues its basis, upgrading the status of affect in relation to reason. The shift is, again, a consequence of his repudiation of the Cartesian way of imagining human presence in the world – of the deep error in not recognising a human mind and its ideas as a subset among other finite modes of substance.

Within these reversals of a more familiar Cartesian framework, the exercise of reason remains crucial to the good human life. Yet it now enters into different configurations with other aspects of the life of the mind. Just how radical that shift is emerges in Spinoza's treatment of 'wonder' – traditionally regarded in Western philosophy as central to the pursuit of knowledge.

Spinoza on Wonder

An initially surprising consequence of Spinoza's principles for the classification of specific affects is that wonder is for him strictly not an affect at all. It involves a fixity in the mind – a pause in its activity. Hence, it fails to satisfy Spinoza's definition of affects in terms of transitions in mental activity. 'Wonder is an imagination of a thing in which the Mind remains fixed because this singular imagination has no connection with the others' (EIII Definitions of the Affects [after EIIIP59], Sec. IV). Wonder, he goes on to explain, is not an affect but rather 'a distraction of the Mind', which does not arise from any positive cause but 'only from the fact that there is no cause determining the Mind to pass from regarding one thing to thinking of others' (EIII Definitions of the Affects Sec. IV, Exp.).

If wonder is not an affect, why consider it at all in describing specific emotions? Spinoza explains that he nonetheless includes it in his listing of the affects because others have made it prominent. Amongst those 'others' is Descartes, who treated wonder as 'the first of all the passions', in his *Passions of the Soul*.[12]

There is more at stake here than an unaccustomed concession, on Spinoza's part, to conformity. Notwithstanding its failure to satisfy his own definition of the affects, wonder is an important thread throughout his treatment of the mind's 'vacillations'. Its presence haunts his other descriptions of specific emotions, their inter-relations and their transformation.

In its stasis, wonder illuminates the vacillation between contraries, which Spinoza sees as arising from a human mind's immersion in the totality of its world. Where the mind is confronted by singularity, it fails to find something in common between different deliverances of the imagination. 'This affection of the Mind, or this imagination of a singular thing, insofar as it is alone in the Mind, is called Wonder' (EIIIP52Schol.).

[12] Descartes 1985: 350 (Part Two, Sec. 53).

Spinoza's treatment of wonder highlights that for him fixity and fluctuation belong together – in the same story of inherent changeability in minds tossed by contrary forces.[13] Wonder, construed as a 'distraction of the mind', is caught up in those fluctuations, combining with a wide range of specific affects to produce new ones. Aroused by fear, wonder yields consternation. Directed to another person's anger, it yields dread. Joined to love, it yields devotion.

Wonder is for Spinoza a crucial presence in the mind's ongoing striving for better understanding. It is a close companion of imagination, which – as he previously stressed in *Ethics II* – strives to encompass 'those things that increase or aid the Body's power of acting' (*EIIIP12*). In that ongoing struggle, the mind – as far as it can – avoids imagining 'those things that diminish or restrain its or the Body's power' (*EIIIP13Cor.*).

The fixity of the imagination, which is for Spinoza the core of wonder, arises from inability to move from the apprehension of singularity to finding commonalities. Singularity elicits wonder. As that stasis subsides with increased familiarity, the mind manages to move on, making the connections which ground the formation of the 'common notions' of reason.

On Spinoza's account, wonder itself undergoes transformation; and its transformations yield new emotions – as when love turns it to devotion. However, the initial 'distraction' of wonder can also give way to a range of more negative conditions – once the mind becomes more inclined to focus on what the object has in common with other things. Thus, as we become more familiar with something at which we wondered, the condition can turn to disdain. That, in turn, can yield mockery (*EIIIP52Schol.*). Wonder can also turn to indifference. Where we cease to see another's virtues as peculiarly his – rather than as 'common to our nature' – the demise of wonder brings a different kind of shift in emotion. We no longer venerate or envy him for his virtues – 'any more than we envy trees their height, or lions their strength' (*EIIIP55Schol.*).

---

[13] I discuss Spinoza's treatment of wonder, and its contrasts with that of Descartes, more fully in Lloyd 2018a: 30–51.

In this mix of positive and negative transformations, wonder emerges as a focal point in a mind's shifts between stasis and movement. Spinoza celebrates it for its connections with a mind's thoughtful, inquiring responses to the world. It brings a pause in thought, out of which emerges a renewed search for commonalities. In the longer term, wonder strengthens understanding rather than diminishing it. The blocked pathway to better understanding becomes an impetus for fresh thinking – finding new ways forward.

Wonder, as well as contributing to better theoretical understanding, is also significant in Spinoza's broader version of the well-lived human life. On his account, a mind's continuing to thrive demands an ongoing effort to recall and imagine what will enhance its own power of acting – in the face of contrary forces that might subdue that power. Wonder is crucial in that ongoing effort of a mind to persist and to thrive, through exercising its own power within the totality of the finite modes of substance.

In Spinoza's analysis of wonder as a quasi affect, a picture emerges of the human mind as an agitated confluence of processes, among which it strives – through the cultivation and the guidance of reason – for a deeper understanding of its own presence in the world. Reason, imagination and emotion are inextricably involved in that ongoing exercise of the powers of the human mind. For Spinoza, reasoning – significant though it is in human life – is itself reliant on the felt awareness of body in imagination. It is also reliant on the understanding of a mind's own transitions in activity, which are for Spinoza – by definition – affects.

For Spinoza the power of reason depends on its interconnections with those other mental processes which later 'rationalism' regarded as lesser than – or subservient to – reason. Again, Spinoza's version of reason is framed by the inclusion of human minds within the wholeness of Nature. From a Spinozist perspective, then, it is not surprising that wonder should now so often accompany insights into the natural world that come with a deeper understanding of climate change.

Against this background of Spinoza's general approach to the affects, and the principles governing his classifications of them, it is illuminating to now look closely at what emerges in *Ethics III* about those emotions that have figured more directly in contemporary climate discussion – hope, fear and grief.

Hope, Fear and Grief: A Spinozist Perspective

In the definitions of the affects in *Ethics III*, hope and fear occupy adjoining positions, with Spinoza stressing their interconnection. 'It follows from their Definitions that there is neither Hope without Fear nor Fear without Hope' (EIII, Definitions of the Affects [after EIIIP59] Sec. XIII Exp.). The point may seem trivial. In a state of fear, we hope for deliverance; and our hopes seem inevitably to summon up fear of those hopes being unfulfilled – or perhaps of possible loss of what they do deliver. There is a shadowing relationship between hope and fear, which seems a feature of how the concepts work.

Spinoza's recognition of the interconnection is neither surprising nor original. As Edwin Curley points out, in a footnote to his translation of Spinoza's 'Explanation' of his Definitions, Seneca made the same observation in one of his *Moral Epistles*.[14] In the passage echoed by Spinoza, Seneca elaborated the point through a striking – though not altogether illuminating – metaphor. Just as the same chain binds both prisoner and guard, he says, so hope and fear – though they are so unlike – march together. Fear trails after hope. The imagery of chains and shackles is not crucial to the conceptual point. Yet it does serve to strengthen the cautionary note about human hopes which was for Seneca the most important message.

Within the frame of a severe form of Stoicism, the interconnection of hope and fear has consequences for human well-being. Seneca's intent was to expose the seductive allure of hope by drawing attention to the fear that must follow in its wake – the shackled prisoner, shuffling after the guard to whom he is chained. For Seneca the important point here is the folly of human desire. To live without being disturbed by fear demands surrendering desire and the hopes associated with it. His conclusion is: cease to hope and you will also cease to fear.

[14] Curley 1985: 534.

There is an implicit reference to the future in Seneca's treatment of hope. He relates the vulnerabilities of hope to a mind's being in suspense – fretted by looking forward to the future. Although fear is also directed to the future, the cautionary note rings more truly in the case of hope. After all, surrendering one's hopes in order to avoid fear seems somewhat more plausible than giving up one's fears in order to avoid hope.

Despite many resonances of Stoicism throughout his works, Spinoza does not share Seneca's pessimism about human desire; and he has a much more positive attitude to emotion, more generally. Yet there are lingering echoes of Seneca in his emphasis on the interconnections of hope and fear. It allows him to move with apparent ease from arguments about the one to conclusions about the other. It is in relation to hope, rather than fear, that the echoes from Stoicism are strongest. However, Spinoza's treatment of hope is significantly different from Seneca's – in ways that raise some interesting issues in the context of contemporary anxieties about the human future.

In his basic definitions and descriptions of the affects in *Ethics III*, Spinoza says of hope that it is 'an inconstant Joy, born of the idea of a future or past thing whose outcome we to some extent doubt' (EIII, Definitions of the Affects [after EIIIP59], Sec. XII). And, in tandem, at Section XIII: 'Fear is an inconstant Sadness, born of the idea of a future or past thing whose outcome we to some extent doubt'.

That reference to past as well as future did not feature in Seneca's discussion. Its inclusion in Spinoza's Definitions may well seem counterintuitive. We can hope or fear that something may have already happened or not happened – in circumstances in which we do not as yet know what Spinoza calls its 'outcome'. Yet that locution seems to be secondary or derivative. A past event, considered in itself, seems to lie beyond human capacity to influence or alter things. So, what is already past seems beyond hope. Likewise, an event – once it is known to be past – seems to cease being an object of fear. It may perhaps become instead an appropriate object of grief, regret or anger.

To see past events as plausible objects of hope or fear, it seems necessary to recast their description, shifting the object of the emotion to a future discovery of a truth about the past. There is a strangeness here – of which more will emerge later in the *Ethics* – which relates, more generally, to Spinoza's approach to the human experience of time. The format of the *Ethics* – its presentations in an array of axioms, definitions, propositions and demonstrations – is better fitted to the enunciation of timeless truths than to subtle nuances of tense distinctions.

Spinoza proclaimed, in the Preface to *Ethics III*, his intention to deal with human affects in the same manner as lines, planes and bodies. He is now, in his listing of specific affects, offering definitions – rather than phenomenological descriptions – of hope and fear. Yet something important to the human experience of hope seems to have gone missing in his emphasis on its symmetry with fear. Although fear resembles hope in its apparent lack of reference to the past, it can surely be directed to an object manifestly present – even if that also involves the consideration of future harm. Hope, in contrast – as Voltaire saw clearly – seems to have an inherent direction to the future.

The strangeness of this apparent disregard of hope's distinctive connection with futurity becomes more striking when Spinoza moves on to definitions of specific affects related to hope and fear. Hope plus removal of doubt yields confidence, which he defines as 'a Joy born of the idea of a future or past thing, concerning which the cause of doubting has been removed' (*EIII*, Definitions of the Affects [after *EIIIP59*], Sec. XIV). And, again in tandem: despair is 'a Sadness born of the idea of a future or past thing concerning which the cause of doubting has been removed' (*EIII*, Definitions of the Affects [after *EIIIP59*], Sec. XV). He continues: 'Confidence, therefore is born of Hope and Despair of Fear, when the cause of doubt concerning the thing's outcome is removed' (*EIII*, Definitions of the Affects [after *EIIIP59*], Sec. XV Exp.).

The reintroduction of the theme of doubt into these definitions is noteworthy. Spinoza's prior treatment of the vacillations of doubt – as key to understanding the general nature of the affects – here seems to be driving the definitions of specific emotions. Intuitively, though, the resulting divisions seem to have gone awry. Surely, despair belongs not with fear, but with hope – opposites, yet somehow belonging in the same territory.

From the common experience of emotions, it is not clear that the removal of doubt from fear necessarily brings despair. In contemporary locutions, the removal of doubt can often be associated with relief – even with resurgence of hope, through transition out of the anxious paralysis of 'not-knowing'. 'At least, I now know', people say, when given a definitive diagnosis which ends prolonged uncertainty.

There is strangeness, too, in the notion that the removal of doubt turns hope into confidence. It is true that confidence evokes a stronger expectation than mere hope. Yet it may well seem odd to describe confidence as 'born of hope' – as if somehow the one condition unfolds into the other, once doubt is removed.

Futurity itself seems to vanish in these definitions – as if it was never quite there in the first place. Hope seems to have become an ephemeral shadow cast by doubt – something which is supposed to give way to some more rational emotion under the light of reason. It is as if hope's association with futurity amounts for Spinoza to nothing more than a temporary mental vacillation, produced by uncertainty.

At this point in Spinoza's discussion of hope, it may well seem that much that is crucial to the human experience of this emotion has slipped through the rigid structure of his Definitions. Yet there are some aspects of his analysis which do seem to yield intimations of its orientation to the future.

In treating hope in tandem with fear, Spinoza highlighted their shared dependence on uncertainty. Yet he also sees them as separated by the strong connections with joy and sadness, respectively. Despite its association with thought of an uncertain future outcome, he saw hope as involving a wavering anticipation of joy, in the midst of uncertainty. That can be seen as connecting hope with the central concept he calls conatus, which, for a mind, resides in the ongoing effort to understand – to apprehend itself ever better in relation to the totality of being.

In thus connecting hope – through joy – with the essence of a human mind, Spinoza offers not so much a reason for hope, as an insight into its preconditions. It is as if, in experiencing and enacting hope, a mind apprehends the onward movement – the struggle to persist – of life itself. Hope carries an anticipation of well-being that is not derived from belief in an assured outcome.

Its inherent connection with joy thus gives Spinozist hope a positive role in human lives, notwithstanding its associations with uncertainty. Despite the text's apparent indifference to the explicit thought of futurity, those tantalising connections between hope and joy, between joy and desire – and between all of them and conatus, as persistence in being – form a cluster of concepts which carry a sense of orientation towards the future.

We will see more fully later, having considered what comes in *Ethics IV* and *V*, how Spinoza's treatment of the collective aspects of hope and fear bear more fully on the sense of futurity. In relation to climate change grief – and its strange connections with hope – Spinoza seems more distant from contemporary emotional response. Grief does not rate a specific mention among his definitions of the affects in *Ethics III*. However, it seems clear that he would have associated it with sadness – and hence with a mind's negative transitions into passivity. This accords with the resonances in his thought of ancient Stoic themes of vulnerability through attachment to things readily lost.

As we have seen, Spinoza's own version of detachment is centred not on the negativity of potential loss, but rather on the powerful affect of joy – a stronger 'force for existing' than any negative passion. Yet the close connections between grief and sadness seem to rule out any possibility that he might have allowed that grief and hope might be collaborators rather than enemies.

It also seems that Spinoza's treatment of the affects could have made little sense of the notion that grief might arise, not so much from potential loss at a future time, but rather from the loss of the very sense of futurity. The future does not seem to figure in his reflections, except as a negative distraction from proper rational concern with the present. Indeed, as we will see later, in *Ethics IV* he suggests that reason is indifferent to the passage of time. 'Insofar as the Mind conceives things from the dictate of reason, it is affected in the same way, whether the idea is of a future or a past thing, or of a present one' (EIVP62Dem.).

Spinoza's endorsement of detachment from the vicissitudes of temporal experience does seem to echo at least some elements of a severe version of Stoicism, in which resistance to the ravages of grief seems to come at the expense of joy in human connection. To avoid the vulnerability can also be to surrender the joy. Spinoza's explicit discussion of specific affects may seem to leave little room for appreciation of the wrenching sense of loss of what has most mattered in the past, which is at the heart of grief.

In the next chapter, it will nonetheless become clear that Spinoza's distinctive integration of understanding, imagination and affect opens space for new insight into the complex layering of thought and emotion that suffuses current responses to climate change.

4

The Power of the Human Mind

Ethics IV and V were written some time after *Ethics* I–III, with Spinoza's work on the *Theological-Political Treatise* intervening. The completed *Ethics* was published only after his death in 1677. Its later parts reflect the content of the previously published *Theological-Political Treatise*, although they are less explicitly concerned with political themes. In the treatment of the role of the affects in *Ethics* IV, there is a shift in emphasis from *Ethics* III – from theoretical understanding of emotions towards concern with ways in which they play out in collective aspects of human lives.

In that new context, Spinoza's earlier analyses of hope and fear take on a more political orientation. There is, nonetheless, continuity in the trajectory of Spinoza's thought. He remains concerned with the interactions of reason, imagination and emotion, against the background of his central themes: the embodiment of human minds and their inclusion in the totality of finite modes of substance. The Preface and early sections of *Ethics* IV reiterate those themes, providing a frame for discussion of ways in which the powers of human minds within Nature are limited.

Spinoza's repudiation of the Cartesian model of human knowing is again at play in *Ethics* IV. However, he is at pains also to challenge what he sees as broader misconceptions of the relations between human minds and the rest of Nature. Here, the appeal of his philosophy for twentieth-century 'deep ecology' takes on new significance in the context of contemporary climate change issues.

'Bondage' and Human Goodness

Spinoza's central concern in *Ethics IV*, as he boldly states at the opening of its Preface, is with the nature of human bondage – the condition in which a mind lacks the power to moderate and restrain the power of its affects, living instead under the control of fortune. To understand that limited power within Nature, he must, he says, first repudiate the notion that human beings should 'look to Nature' as a model for human good or evil, perfection or imperfection.

Spinoza takes himself to have already established that God-or-Nature neither exists for a purpose nor acts for the sake of ends. Hence, it provides no model for how human beings should live. To think otherwise, he insists, is to project what is good for human beings – what satisfies their desires – onto Nature as a whole. Those who do so then foolishly treat that idealised Nature as a guide for their own actions.

Spinoza is also at pains in the Preface to warn that his own treatment of human 'power of acting' is not meant to suggest that there is, between different parts of Nature, any difference in degree of perfection. Out of all this comes a striking summation of the contrast between human and non-human; they have their own distinctive powers and pleasures. 'A horse is destroyed as much if it is changed into a man as if it is changed into an insect' (EIVPreface).

For Spinoza, there is no absolute goodness or badness to be ascribed to those things of which human beings avail themselves in their efforts to continue to exist and to thrive. Nor are their own passions absolutely either good or bad. They are to be evaluated in terms of the role they play in the ongoing effort to persist within a world in which human beings, like other things, are subject to constant change. Human goodness is to be understood through human well-being; but that well-being is not construed in terms of a perfection inscribed in Nature. Nor is it to be regarded as an external reward for good behaviour.

Spinoza's philosophy does not offer assurance of a world rationally ordered towards ends that are ultimately good for humanity. Human beings are for him inserted into a totality of finite processes, which have no inherent bearing on what may best serve their individual or collective well-being. Human powers are integrated – for better or worse – into the powers of the rest of Nature.

With that framework in place, Spinoza proceeds to develop his own treatment of the limited powers that human minds have within Nature. The key concept here is desire, which is presented as the essence of human striving to persist in existence. As he has already said in *Ethics III*, it is not the case that human beings desire things because those things are good; things are good because human beings desire them.

The consideration of the power of affects is Spinoza's main focus of *Ethics IV*. Yet, in understanding that power, the role of imagination is again front and centre; and at the core of that role is, once again, the active power of ideas themselves to remove or 'exclude' one another. Underlying Spinoza's treatment of the powers of the mind in relation to its passions is his earlier analysis of error – the upshot of which he now reiterates: 'Nothing positive which a false idea has is removed by the presence of the true insofar as it is true' (EIVP1).

Spinoza insists again that the power struggle between ideas is enacted through operations of imagination:

> For an imagination is an idea which indicates the present constitution of the human Body more than the nature of an external body – not distinctly, of course, but confusedly. This is how it happens that the Mind is said to err. (EIVP1Schol.)

The crucial point here is something he takes himself to have already shown against the Cartesians: ideas are not set aside through an exercise of will. They are set aside because 'there occur others, stronger than them, which exclude the present existence of the things we imagine' (EIVP1Schol.).

Spinoza's previous definitions of 'adequacy' and 'inadequacy' in ideas now come into play again in relation to the power of the affects. The power of human beings, he observes, is 'infinitely surpassed by the power of external causes' (EIVP3Dem.). The reference to 'external' causes echoes the *Ethics III* definition of human freedom in terms of 'adequacy': free acts are those that can be understood through the mind's own nature. Insofar as its ideas are adequate, a mind is itself the cause of its own activity. Spinoza now observes that, since human beings are inexorably part of Nature, that freedom is always at risk. For it is impossible that human beings should avoid undergoing changes of which the cause cannot be explained through their own nature alone (EIVP4Dem.).

Spinoza's account of human knowledge and error thus frames his treatment of human reason's engagement with the affects – and of what can be expected from that engagement. His previous conclusions about reason's relations with imagination are now, throughout *Ethics IV*, interwoven with his account of the interrelations of imagination and emotion.

Against that background, Spinoza is concerned with the power of the rest of Nature over human minds, and with the limitations of reason in resisting that power.

In *Ethics V*, he will go on to consider what human minds can do in resistance – by integrating their individual and collective powers. There, he will sketch a path through – and beyond – reason, by which a mind can gain some measure of freedom within the vagaries of fortune.

Reason and the Passions

According to Spinoza, the mind does not err from the mere fact that it imagines. So too, human reason does not have power over the affects by the mere presence to it of truth. 'No affect can be restrained by the true knowledge of good and evil insofar as it is true, but only insofar as it is considered as an affect' (EIVP14). Mere knowledge of what is good does not enable a mind to free itself from the bondage of negative passions. That release happens through the connection of understanding with joy – the positive affect, which Spinoza has defined in terms of a mind's transition to greater activity.

The conflict between reason and the passions is thus for Spinoza not a power struggle between rival faculties. It is a struggle between a mind's active and passive affects – understood in terms of 'adequate' and 'inadequate' ideas of transition to greater or less mental activity. Understanding is part of that story only inasmuch as it is itself imbued with affect.

The contrasts between activity and passivity here are multi-layered. A passion can involve an inadequate idea of transition to greater activity; and an active affect can involve an adequate idea of transition to lesser activity. In thus explicating the limited power of the mind's understanding within Nature, Spinoza offers a subtle and illuminating treatment of human reason. We will see later that it has important ramifications for contemporary ways of thinking in the context of climate change.

In Spinoza's philosophy, human minds, like other individual finite modes, strive to persist in existence. Reason is the expression of that striving in adequate understanding. 'What we strive for from reason is nothing but understanding; nor does the Mind, insofar as it uses reason, judge anything else useful to itself except what leads to understanding' (EIVP26). For the essence of reason is 'nothing but our Mind, insofar as it understands clearly and distinctly' (EIVP26Dem.).

Spinoza has already argued, in *Ethics II*, that insofar as it understands adequately, the human mind is included as an idea in the 'mind of God' – the totality of thought, in which all ideas are 'adequate'. From the definitions in *Ethics IV*, such a mind is also 'free'. However, a human mind inevitably includes also 'inadequate' ideas, which result, not from its own activity, but from its body being acted upon by other things. Since it exists only as the idea of a body existing within the totality of finite modes, and is hence subject to being changed by other bodies, a mind cannot be absolutely free. Its freedom – and its inclusion in the 'mind of God' – apply to it only, in Spinoza's recurring locution, 'insofar as' it is construed as having 'adequate' ideas.

That 'insofar as' locution glides over the issue of how best to articulate the relations between two such different ways of construing a human mind – as an adequate idea in 'the mind of God', and as a conglomerate of ideas which are, for the most part, 'inadequate'. It may seem that Spinoza has engaged in an elaborate reconstruction of a hierarchical relation between reason – the provenance of 'adequate' ideas – and a residue of 'inadequate' ideas, which bind the mind to the rest of the world. Has he led his readers, by a circuitous route, just to a new model of a two-tiered mind – divided between the 'adequate' ideas of reason and the 'inadequate' ideas of sense or imagination?

If that were so, it would be a disappointing outcome – from the perspective of contemporary readers, wanting to draw on Spinoza for aid in rethinking human relations with the rest of Nature. Capacity for reason, after all, has been the pivot on which has turned the belief in human supremacy over mere Nature. However, to read Spinoza's treatment of reason as just another version of that familiar refrain would be, again, to ignore his two central theses about human minds – their inherent embodiment, and their consequent immersion in the whole of Nature. It would be, again, to think of human minds along the Cartesian model of mind and thought, which Spinoza has rejected.

Grasping the radical shift of thought here, and its contemporary relevance, involves starting from a sense of the wholeness of Nature, glimpsed from within that totality – through the confusion of felt awareness of an ever-changing human body. That is the context for Spinoza's insistence, throughout *Ethics IV*, on the inherently limited powers of human minds.

In *Ethics V*, Spinoza will offer a complementary treatment of the powers that a human mind does nonetheless possess. However, before turning to what lies beyond reason, he must first address more fully the powers of reason within Nature. In doing so, he considers also the powers of non-human species, which do not have the capacity to 'live by reason'. Here we see again those apparently negative views on human–non-human relations which proved controversial in discussions of Spinoza in twentieth-century Environmental Philosophy.

'Powers and Pleasures' Within Nature

At the core of Spinoza's version of human goodness is his account of what is specifically to the advantage of human beings. That sounds very much a human-centred approach to relations between human and non-human. There are, however, some important differences between Spinoza's version of the pursuit of human 'advantage' and the associations of 'self-interest' – a more familiar term which, unsurprisingly, is seen as fostering indifference to the rights or needs of non-human parts of Nature.

Spinoza's version of seeking the advantage of what is human demands a collective pursuit of human well-being, centred on the improvement of understanding:

> To man ... there is nothing more useful than man. Man, I say, can wish for nothing more helpful to the preservation of his being than that all should so agree in all things that the Minds and Bodies of all would compose, as it were, one Mind and one Body; that all should strive together, as far as they can, to preserve their being; and that all, together, should seek for themselves the common advantage of all. (EIVP18Schol.)

Spinoza associates that 'common advantage' directly with human reason:

> It is not by accident that man's greatest good is common to all; rather, it arises from the very nature of reason, because it is deduced from the very essence of man, insofar as [that essence] is defined by reason, and because man could neither be nor be conceived if he did not have the power to enjoy this greatest good. (EIVP36Schol.)

For Spinoza the pursuit of individual advantage – rather than encouraging competition or rivalry – demands collaboration between human beings. He elaborates on the value of collective pursuit of well-being in his account of friendship as the true foundation of a well-functioning state – a theme that is more fully developed in his political writings. In the collaborations epitomised in friendship, the powers of each individual are strengthened. That forms the basis for a view of the non-human which can sound, disconcertingly, similar to familiar notions of human supremacy within Nature:

> The rational principle of seeking our own advantage teaches us the necessity of joining with men, but not with the lower

animals, or with things whose nature is different from human nature. We have the same right against them that they have against us. Indeed, because the right of each one is defined by his virtue, or power, men have a far greater right against the lower animals than they have against men. (EIVP37Schol.1)

Spinoza concludes that in 'seeking our own advantage' human beings may use those non-human beings at our pleasure, and treat them as is most convenient for us. 'For they do not agree in nature with us, and their affects are different in nature from human affects.' To think otherwise in relation to animals, he insists, is 'based more on empty superstition and unmanly compassion than sound reason' (EIVP37Schol.1).

Against the background of his earlier affirmation of the 'powers and pleasures' of different species – illustrated in the distinctive joys and perfection of horses – the apparent 'speciesism' of the conclusion he now draws may be surprising. Descartes had argued, notoriously, that animals were best seen as automata, rather than as sentient beings. Spinoza, in contrast, indicates that he is well aware that non-human creatures have sensations. Indeed he presents his argument as based on the recognition that they 'do not agree in nature with us, and their affects are different in nature from human affects' (EIVP37Schol.1).

Spinoza's views on 'the lower animals' are grounded in the emphasis he has consistently placed on the specific nature and operations of human minds. He makes the point explicit in a later passage: 'Any singular thing whose nature is entirely different from ours can neither aid nor restrain our power of acting, and absolutely, no thing can be either good or evil for us, unless it has something in common with us' (EIVP29).

Spinoza's conclusions can indeed sound similar to more familiar privileging of human interests against the interests of other species. Yet they have a very different conceptual basis. His focus and emphasis is on human commonalities – as distinct from the 'powers and pleasures' of other beings. What humans have in common facilitates – and is enhanced by – the collective pursuit of 'goods' associated with the cultivation of reason. Again, 'goodness' is here to be understood as what contributes to human well-being; and that in turn is understood in terms of the collective strengthening of the powers exercised by human beings in understanding themselves, other things and God.

On Spinoza's account, passions divide human beings, whereas reason unites them. The necessity of collective pursuit of the common good; the role of friendship in the foundation of political organisation; the place of reason in that shared pursuit; and humans' pursuit of what is to the advantage of their own species: – all these things, for him, reflect the embodiment of human minds within the totality of Nature. He sees that whole cluster of themes as grounded in his insistence that human beings do not occupy a special terrain within Nature; that they are subject to the same necessities that govern other things. Shared reason enables human thriving only within those necessities, from which there is no possible exemption.

In the context of contemporary consideration of climate change issues, the route by which Spinoza reaches his conclusions about human relations with other species is more significant than the views themselves. Greater understanding of bodily structure and behaviour can yield more nuanced differentiations between humans and non-human species, allowing for greater appreciation of commonalities; and insights from modern ecology have yielded a rich understanding of the interdependent thriving of different species.

Change in the conditions of existence for all species, within a finite natural world, can mean that the application of a conceptual framework has a different upshot in a context later than that in which it was formulated. Collective pursuit of what contributes to human well-being can no longer be construed as sharply separated out from the conditions under which other species thrive.

Spinoza offers a model of human thought – and of human well-being – that is grounded in denying the separation of human life from the necessities governing the rest of Nature. The conclusions he draws for the treatment of other species may look superficially the same as those grounded in the separatism that flows from the Cartesian model which he repudiated. Yet, in a changing world, the upshot of his philosophy is different. It can more readily adapt to increased understanding of species commonalities across difference, as well as to changing conditions that affect all species.

Reason and the Non-rational: The Ideal and the Real

Spinoza does not seek to justify an alliance of human beings as such – whatever their collective capacities and deficiencies – against the rest of Nature. For him, the capacities associated with reason do not comprise all that is involved in human sameness. 'Insofar as men are subject to passions, they cannot be said to agree in nature' (EIVP32).

There is an important point here, which illuminates Spinoza's version of reason. It is not in virtue of some underlying property, possessed by all human beings, that they can be said to share a common nature. On Spinoza's approach, commonalities emerge in the way humans live and respond to one another. 'Only insofar as men live according to the guidance of reason, must they always agree in nature' (EIVP35). Insofar as they are 'torn by affects which are passions', they can be 'different in nature' and 'contrary to one another' (EIVP35Dem.).

Spinoza's way of thinking of 'agreement in nature' has some consequences that may seem counterintuitive. They arise from his earlier insistence, in *Ethics II*, that all human beings have an adequate understanding of God (EII P47). He now equates that understanding of God with the greatest good for human beings, observing that it is 'not by accident that man's greatest good is common to all'. Rather, 'it arises from the very nature of reason' – deduced 'from the very essence of man, insofar as [that essence] is defined by reason'. Summing up that array of connections between reason, human essence and the 'greatest good', Spinoza concludes: '[M]an could neither be nor be conceived if he did not have the power to enjoy this greatest good. For it pertains to the essence of the human Mind to have an adequate knowledge of God's eternal and infinite essence' (EIVP36Schol.).

Clearly, there are tensions here. Living under the guidance of reason is for Spinoza the greatest of human goods, derived from the very essence of the human mind. Yet the upshot of *Ethics IV*, as a whole, is that human beings are 'subject to the affects, which far surpass man's power, or virtue' (EIVP37Schol.2). Such, for Spinoza, is the dilemma of human life.

Spinoza's recognition of the gap between the real and the ideal may sound like a familiar lament of human weakness in knowing the good, while yet failing to act consistently with that knowledge. Yet it has a crucially different emphasis. His ideal of following the 'guidance of reason' is not to be construed as a norm, from which there are unfortunate and deplorable lapses. It is a possibility, glimpsed from within the normal ebb and flow of human passions. He insists that those passions themselves are not to be disdained or mocked as blameable vice or sin. They are part of the fluctuating totality of things, in which human minds find their only true good in the collaborative effort to reach ever better understanding.

Out of the insight that all things – including human passions – happen from the necessities of Nature, Spinoza has developed a distinctive approach to human weakness and folly:

> He who rightly knows that all things flow from the necessity of the divine nature, and happen according to the eternal laws and rules of nature, will surely find nothing worthy of Hate, Mockery or Disdain, nor anyone whom he will pity. Instead he will strive, as far as human virtue allows, to act well, as they say, and rejoice. (EIVP50Schol.)

In insisting on not finding anyone 'pitiable', it is not Spinoza's intention to encourage the withholding of sympathy from fellow human beings. On the contrary, he is quick to add that one who is moved to aid others neither by reason nor by pity is rightly called inhuman. 'For he seems to be unlike a man' (EIVP50Schol.). The well-lived human life, as it is here envisaged, is one centred on the cultivation of positive, rather than negative affects – while yet acknowledging the necessities that far surpass human powers.

To live under the guidance of reason is for Spinoza not a matter of following external impositions. It is to live in accordance with one's own nature – as understood through collaboration with likeminded others. Such lives are for him grounded in positive affects – related to joy, rather than sadness. His definitions and demonstrations of the nature of the various affects are meant to show that 'things which bring it about that men live harmoniously, at the same time bring it about that they live in accordance to the guidance of reason' (EIVP40Dem.). Hence, human virtue is expressed in sociable 'laughter and joking', rather than in despondency. 'The greater the Joy with which we are affected, the greater the perfection to which we pass, i.e. the more we must participate in the divine nature' (EIVP45Schol.).

This version of the ideals associated with reason enacts Spinoza's insistence on the truth of human embodiment within Nature. In a much-quoted passage, he observes:

> It is the part of a wise man, I say, to refresh and restore himself in moderation with pleasant food and drink, with scents, with the beauty of green plants, with decoration, music, sports, the theatre, and other things of this kind, which anyone can use without injury to another. For the human Body is composed of a great many parts of different natures, which constantly require new and varied nourishment, so that the whole Body may be equally capable of undertaking the things which can follow from its nature, and hence, so that the Mind also may be equally capable of understanding many things. (EIVP45Schol.)

Spinoza's emphasis on joy grounds a version of the well-lived life that is in some ways the antithesis of the distrust of emotion associated with austere forms of Stoicism. It is interesting to note also here that the emphasis on joy ensures that wonder – that condition which is at play throughout his treatment of the affects, without itself satisfying their definition – has a vibrant presence in his depiction of the good human life. Even where human affects do not indicate human power, he says, they 'at least indicate the power and skill of nature, no less than many other things we wonder at and take pleasure in contemplating' (EIVP57Schol.).

For Spinoza, Nature is not imbued with purpose. Yet to deny the presence of purpose in the natural world is not to cease to find in it objects of wonder, which the well-functioning mind takes pleasure in contemplating and trying to understand. On the contrary, as he has insisted, it allows human passions themselves to become objects of pleasurable contemplation and understanding, rather than derision.

It is also worth noting, in passing, that Spinoza's version of doubt has some affinities with his treatment of wonder as involving a vacillation or 'distraction' of the mind. The comparison of doubt and wonder is not a central theme of Spinoza's philosophy. Yet he often remarks, in his critiques of rival theorists, that they 'do not wonder at' something – or, more generally, that they 'do not wonder enough'. On his analysis, the capacity for wonder and the capacity for doubt can go together in a mind attuned to truth-seeking.

Spinoza has offered his own version of the ancient adage that the wise and virtuous go on their way rejoicing. What, in this happy story of collective joy, becomes of the passions of hope and fear? Spinoza returns to them in the later sections of *Ethics IV*, with a new orientation towards their collective forms. His discussion there echoes some of what he has had to say in the intervening *Theological-Political Treatise*. What emerges about hope can yield further insight into climate change emotion in a contemporary context, especially in relation to the changing sense of the future.

Fear, Hope and the Sense of the Future

Spinoza's treatment of hope and fear in *Ethics IV* draws on the interconnections which he takes himself to have demonstrated in *Ethics III*. In keeping with his definitions in *Ethics IV*, neither hope nor fear can be regarded as unqualified human goods, for both are implicated in sadness. In the case of fear, the sadness is direct. However, since there is no hope without fear, hope also is caught up in fear's impeding of mental activity; and that obstruction of activity is, by Spinoza's definition, sadness.

The connection of fear and hope to sadness is accentuated by their inevitable association with uncertainty, which Spinoza associates with a lack of power within the mind. Thus, he sees even confidence – a related positive affect – as shadowed by a preceding sadness arising from lack of certainty. It can seem a bleak picture of hope, though it fits neatly with Spinoza's emphasis on the relative stability to be gained from the cultivation of reason.

The more we strive to live according to the guidance of reason, the more we strive to depend less on Hope, to free ourselves from Fear, to conquer fortune as much as we can, and to direct our actions by the certain counsel of reason. (EIVP47Schol.)

Any suggestion that might be seen here of a repudiation of hope is tempered by Spinoza's constant reiteration that an embodied mind's inclusion in the totality of Nature makes it inevitable that it will be subject to the passions – and hence to the vagaries of fortune. Again, to be subject to hope and fear is for Spinoza not a regrettable aberration; it is the human condition. Yet, within the framing necessities of the whole of Nature, he finds the possibility of attaining a precarious freedom. Spinoza argues that, towards that end, there is more to be gained from hope than from fear.

In this treatment of hope and fear – and of imagining what it might be to live without them – Spinoza again emphasises the importance of understanding human weakness, rather than deriding it, and of not withholding fellow-feeling. In the consideration of human collectivities, especially, the usefulness of these emotions becomes apparent, for the goal of having human beings live ever harmoniously together under the guidance of reason is unattainable.

Because human beings rarely live from the 'dictates of reason', hope and fear bring more advantage than disadvantage. Adopting, for the sake of argument, the negative language of his opponents, Spinoza suggests that, since human beings 'sin', the 'weak-minded' should do so in that direction, rather than neither fearing nor hoping for anything. He argues also that it is wise for those in authority to recognise the force of these passions. 'The mob is terrifying, if unafraid' (EIVP54Schol.). Yet, hope's direct association with joy – strengthened in interaction with fellow human beings – means that the wise governor will seek to cultivate it, rather than fear, in those governed. The general cultivation of reason is directed to becoming less dependent on hope, rather than free of it.

Spinoza's discussion in *Ethics IV* thus allows a degree of separation between hope and fear, which seemed absent from his earlier definitions in *Ethics III*. Fear is for him a negative passion, involving transition to passivity – in contrast to the greater activity of mind associated with joy and desire. 'He who is guided by Fear, and does good to avoid evil, is not guided by reason' (EIVP63). Hope, in contrast, seems to have at least some prospect of playing a constructive role in living well, both individually and collectively. Yet, despite his more positive view of hope in *Ethics IV*, there are still muted echoes of severe Stoic disdain of its connections with uncertainty.

It is illuminating here to compare Spinoza's attitudes towards hope in *Ethics IV* with Voltaire's celebration of it. Like Voltaire, Spinoza sees hope as involving an orientation towards the future. To live without concern for the future would be to live without hope. However, as we saw earlier, Spinoza – unlike Voltaire – does not equate the absence of hope with despair. He contrasts the condition of hope with a calm detachment, indicative of the power of reason. 'Insofar as the Mind conceives things from the dictate of reason, it is affected equally, whether the idea is of a future or past thing, or of a present one' (EIVP62). He goes on to add in a scholium:

> If we could have adequate knowledge of the duration of things, and determine by reason their times of existing, we would regard future things with the same affect as present ones, and the Mind would want the good it conceived as future just as it wants the good it conceived as present. (EIVP62Schol.)

It may sound as if Spinoza, echoing severe Stoicism, is suggesting that hope, along with all concern with the future, should be shed by those aspiring to live well. Yet, here again, Spinoza is talking of an unattainable goal of reason. There is in fact no possibility of human minds having 'adequate knowledge of the duration of things'. A human mind, because of its positioning within the totality of ideas, can understand the duration of things only inadequately. It becomes clear that Spinoza sees this inevitable inadequacy as arising from the structural inter-relations of human affects with imagination, which 'is not equally affected by an image of a present thing and the image of a future one' (EIVP62Schol.).

On Spinoza's account, reason – considered in itself – is not subject to the fluctuations or vacillations that affect imagination and affect, when confronted with futurity. However that stability of reason, as we have seen, comes at the cost of engagement with singularity. Spinoza now elaborates that cost, bound up with reason's concern with abstractions:

> The true knowledge we have of good and evil is only abstract, or universal . . . And so it is no wonder if the Desire that arises from a knowledge of good and evil, insofar as this looks to the future, can be rather easily restrained by a Desire for the pleasures of the moment. (EIVP62Schol.)

Reason's strength in resisting those immediate pleasures depends on its lack of concern with singularities. There are thus nuances in Spinoza's treatment of the power of reason, which modify his celebration of its power in relation to the affects. There is an interplay of reason and imagination in his version of the mind's power to manage its passions – a constant tension between the abstractness of reason and the concrete particularity of imagination. Again, what is at stake is not a blameworthy aberration or a lamentable lack of perfection. The human tendency to be – for the most part – swayed by concern with the present is, for Spinoza, an inevitable consequence of the fact that human lives unfold not in a realm of abstract universals, but in the fluctuating world of bodily interaction.

Spinoza's analysis of the mind's confrontation with futurity, in *Ethics IV*, draws out the consequences of his previous treatment of the role of imagination in resolving doubt, in earlier parts of the *Ethics*. He explained in *Ethics II*, especially at Proposition 49, that doubt is not to be resolved by methodical inspection of something present before the mind like a picture. He elaborated that point, in *Ethics III*, in the Explanation to his definitions of confidence and despair. The removal of doubt, he said there, happens 'because [a] man imagines that the past or future thing is there, and regards it as present, or because he imagines other things, excluding the existence of the things that put him in doubt' (*E*III, Definitions of the Affects [after P 59], Sec. XV, Exp.).

In the first of those situations, the mind is brought into the thrall of imagined presence, taking what is before it as something real, without doubting it. In the second situation, the thing imagined is 'excluded from existence' by the force of other things, which are actually present. It is that second case – where doubt is removed by the thing imagined being excluded from existence – that now resurfaces in Spinoza's treatment in *Ethics IV* of the management of the passions.

Here, again, readers are confronted with the strangeness of Spinoza's locution of ideas 'excluding one another', which seems to have no ready match in contemporary philosophy. As I mentioned earlier in discussing Spinoza's treatment of doubt, Spinoza's use of this locution is not meant to suggest a considered ruling out of a claim to truth. It does not evoke an exercise of a dominant will over natural propensities within a human mind. In *Ethics IV*, in his treatment of the management of the passions, the locution takes on connotations of a different kind of power struggle. Rather than a conflict between the power of human will and Nature, it has become a struggle between rival forces, competing for continued existence within the totality of being.

Spinoza's treatment of the role of imagination in the dynamics of doubt thus resonates in his account of reason's relations with the affects, yielding a vision of the whole human mind acting within the wholeness of Nature. What is particularly striking here is that the fluctuations or vacillations of imagination do not merely intensify or exacerbate human emotion; they enter into its very nature.

Those fluctuations of imagination play out especially in Spinoza's treatment of the social aspects of collective hope and fear, where the powers of individual minds are strengthened or hindered through their relations with others. His remarks on collective hope and fear in *Ethics IV* echo fuller discussion in his political writings, where it is possible to see more clearly how they might be brought to bear on contemporary responses to climate change.

Spinoza's political writings address issues of religion, governance and intellectual freedom. They contain dark insights into the inter-relations of fear and hope, in a broader context of the manipulation of passions by state power. Those manipulations exploit the passions of 'the superstitious', who then become, as he says in *Ethics IV*, 'generally burdensome and hateful to men' (EIVP63Schol.). Yet he also offers in the political writings a more nuanced treatment of the role of hope in well-lived lives.

The Politics of Hope and Fear

The Preface to the *Theological-Political Treatise* opens with a bleak evocation of the deep unease human beings experience in relation to things that are uncertain, and the fragility of their hold on the steadiness of reason.[1] 'Now they hope for better things; now they fear worse, all for the slightest reasons.' In that mentality, 'the common people' – as Spinoza calls them in this work – 'invent countless things and interpret nature in amazing ways, as if the whole of nature were as crazy as they are'.[2] It is, he says, 'as impossible to save the common people from superstition as it is from fear'.[3]

However, as he also observes in *Ethics IV*, it is not just the people's own mentality that is to be blamed for their wretched condition. Their superstitious hopes and fears are unscrupulously manipulated by those who claim authority over them, while being cunningly intent on maintaining their own status and power.

In contrasting a mentality of hope and fear with the cultivation of reason, in the *Theological-Political Treatise*, one of Spinoza's main targets is the abuse of power by deceptive and self-serving religious zealots, who pose as authoritative interpreters of biblical texts. He suggests that, between those self-styled bearers of divine light and the common people, there is a collusion that takes all alike ever further from access to truth.

Spinoza's critique aims to expose and undermine that collusion, thereby enabling a strategic alliance between genuine religious piety and the free cultivation of reason. He is at the same time intent on defending his own commitment to intellectual freedom against its being wrongly regarded as a threat to the piety and peace of the Dutch Republic.

---

[1] Curley 2016: 66.
[2] Ibid. 66.
[3] Ibid. 75.

There is a clever strategy here in forging new conceptual alliances. Spinoza insists that genuine human knowledge, cultivated through reason, rests on foundations which are common to all. Yet he observes that 'the common people' spurn their own natural knowledge in pursuit of spurious prophetic insights, purveyed by those seeking power. He can then present himself as respecting the claim of ancient prophets to a direct access, through sensitive imagination, to the divine power of God.

For Spinoza, of course, that divine power is not anything supernatural. It is nothing but the totality of powers in the natural world, which are themselves the proper objects of scientific understanding. Yet he shrewdly seeks here, in introducing his *Theological-Political Treatise*, to bring reverence for 'divine revelation' – associated with the prophets – into a strategic alliance with the scientific understanding of Nature.

Spinoza thus offers in the *Theological-Political Treatise* an audacious refiguring of areas of discourse. Divine revelation – accessed by the ancient prophets and enshrined in scripture – is aligned with scientific inquiry into the natural world. He claims, as in *Ethics IV*, that the more human beings come to understand Nature, the greater and more perfect is the knowledge they have of God.

In relation to issues of governance, Spinoza's treatment of hope in the *Theological-Political Treatise* elaborates points he also makes in the *Ethics* about its positive aspects, as against the negative force of fear. No ruler, he observes, can survive long by inspiring fear; most frequently, the people are compelled by the use of fear and hope together. After all, one of the strongest goods they desire is indeed to be freed from fear.

Good government is thus presented as involving a shrewd manipulation of the satisfaction of hope and the anxiety of fear. In Chapter 4, he observes that those who support the laws are provided with what 'the common people most love', while those who would break the laws are threatened with 'what they most fear'. In this way, the legislators 'have tried, as far as they could, to restrain the common people, as you might rein in a horse'.[4]

---

[4] Curley 2016: 127.

Spinoza here allows hope a more positive role than fear in the pursuit of collective well-being. Yet both hope and fear remain associated with a mentality of bondage. He contrasts that condition with the certainty associated with 'the knowledge and love of God'.[5] The dynamics of doubt, which figured in the definitions of hope and fear in earlier parts of the *Ethics*, thus resurface in the treatment of political power in the *Theological-Political Treatise*.

In Spinoza's later *Political Treatise*, which was left unfinished at his death in 1677, there is another interesting shift in the configuration of hope, fear and reason. Here, Spinoza's talk of 'the weak-minded' and of 'the common people' is replaced by talk of 'the multitude'. The shift in terminology may sound to contemporary readers less elitist. However, it also suggests a bleaker picture, in general, of human potential for the cultivation of reason. Susceptibility to error is here more explicitly treated as the normal condition of human life.

That difference in emphasis reflects a deepening of Spinoza's insight into the ramifications of human beings' inclusion in the totality of Nature. In Chapter I of the *Political Treatise*, he observes that those who persuade themselves that a people can be induced to live only in accordance with reason are captive to a myth – dreaming of the 'golden age of the Poets'.[6] Accordingly, he says, 'we must seek the causes and natural foundations of the state, not from the teachings of reason, but from the common nature, or condition, of men'.[7]

In Chapter II of the *Political Treatise*, Spinoza reiterates what he has said in *Ethics IV*: he is concerned with the passions, not as vices, but as properties of human beings. He now argues that understanding these human properties is crucial to governance. He also emphasises seeing human powers within Nature as an expression of the power of God-or-Nature. 'The power by which natural things exist, and so by which they have effects, can't be anything but the eternal power of God itself.'[8]

---

[5] Ibid. 128.
[6] Ibid. 506.
[7] Ibid. 506.
[8] Ibid. 507.

That approach to powers within Nature is now brought to bear directly on political aspects of power. It is significant that, despite his constant affirmation of reason, Spinoza is concerned to stress its limited role – both in a well-lived human life and in issues of governance. He argues that, since human beings are led 'more by blind desire than by reason', their 'natural power, or Right' ought to be defined 'not by reason, but by whatever appetite determines them to act and to strive to preserve themselves'.[9]

Spinoza's aim is not to minimise the power of reason within an integrated wholeness of mind. It is to insist that the desires generated through reason are themselves effects of Nature, displaying the natural force by which human beings persist in being. 'Whether a man is wise or ignorant, he's a part of nature, and whatever determines him to act must be referred to the power of nature, insofar as it can be defined by the nature of this or that man.'[10] Rather than being seen as rightfully dominating Nature, human reason is here itself naturalised.

This naturalisation of reason draws out the consequences of Spinoza's treatment of human freedom in the *Ethics*. Human powers do not arise from a force of free will, which separates them from the rest of Nature. On the contrary, those powers manifest the inclusion of human beings in Nature. 'Whether a man is led by reason or only by desire, he does nothing except according to the laws and rules of nature, i.e. . . ., in accordance with the right of nature'.[11]

In his political writings, Spinoza has refigured the relations between human reason and human passions. In the *Political Treatise*, there is also a refiguration – and, in some ways, a minimising – of the contrast between the wise and the ignorant, which has been at play in his talk of the 'weak-minded' (in *Ethics IV*) and of the 'common people' (in the *Theological-Political Treatise*). He now puts an even stronger emphasis on shared frailty and proneness to error – on the frailty of common humanity, as distinct from the weakness or ignorance of some human beings.

---

[9] Ibid. 508.
[10] Ibid. 509.
[11] Ibid. 509.

That shift in emphasis strengthens Spinoza's nuanced adaptation of old themes of lamentable human weakness in following ideals of reason. 'We conclude, then, that it's not in any one's power to always use reason and be at the highest peak of human freedom – but that nevertheless everyone always strives, so far as he can, to preserve his being.'[12]

In the context of this emphasis on human powers within – rather than against – Nature, hope and fear take on a new significance. They are no longer shadowy presences that serve to intensify the light of reason. They become what is most important to understand about how human collectivities operate, and about how they should be governed. In Chapter III of the *Political Treatise*, he insists on their centrality:

> Both in the natural state and in the civil order, man acts according to the laws of his own nature and looks out for his own advantage. In each situation, I say, man is guided by hope or fear, either to do or not to do, this or that action.[13]

In the *Political Treatise*, Spinoza's earlier talk of 'reining in' a recalcitrant 'common people', who are regrettably not guided by reason, gives way to a stronger emphasis on human vulnerabilities. Amid the 'common fear' and 'common wretchedness' of the human multitude, there arises a shared desire for security – the true basis for a stable civil order, in which human lives can thrive.[14]

With regard to the relative importance of reason and the passions in relation to issues of governance, Spinoza goes even further. He warns that human beings who are not motivated by fear and hope – if such paragons of reason could exist – would be those least of all able to be trusted within a civil order. 'Because those who neither fear nor hope for anything are to that extent their own masters . . . they are . . . enemies of the state, whom it may rightly restrain.'[15] The final upshot of Spinoza's treatment of hope

---

[12] Ibid. 510.
[13] Ibid. 518.
[14] Ibid. 519.
[15] Ibid. 520–1.

and fear is that the security of the state rests ultimately on shared passions, rather than on reason. 'For certainly men are guided by nature to unite in one aim, either because of a common [hope or] a common fear, or because they long to avenge some common loss.'[16]

In Spinoza's political writings, hope move moves further away from fear than was permitted in the tight definitions of *Ethics IV*. Hope's connections with joy make it something to celebrate rather than deplore. In Chapter V of the *Political Treatise*, he observes that 'a free multitude is guided by hope more than by fear, whereas a multitude which has been subjugated is guided more by fear than by hope'. The first 'want to cultivate life'; the second 'care only to avoid death'.[17]

Those remarks echo Spinoza's treatment in *Ethics IV* of the centrality of the power of joy, and of the dependence of reason on affect in managing the passions. In the later sections of the incomplete *Political Treatise*, Spinoza considers the contrasts between appeal to reason and appeal to affects, in the context of threats to collective security – a precondition of well-lived human lives. Here, especially, it is to the 'common affects' that governance must look, rather than to the cultivation of reason alone. In Chapter X, he comments that laws 'can't be unshaken unless they are defended both by reason and by men's common affects; otherwise, if they rest only on the support of reason, they are of course weak and easily overcome'.[18]

Creatures of Myth?

Spinoza's political writings make it clear that for him hope and fear belong in the fabric of the human world – the world of collective human powers, which themselves unavoidably affect and are affected by other powers. It also becomes clear that he sees proneness to passions – as well as proneness to error – as no mere aberration, afflicting the 'weak-minded'. For Spinoza there is no

[16] Ibid. 521.
[17] Ibid. 530.
[18] Ibid. 600.

firm divide between those who pursue the 'freedom of reason' and those who live under the 'bondage' of passions. All human beings fluctuate between the two conditions.

According to Spinoza, free human beings act from reason rather than from fear – desiring the good directly. Yet the figure of the free human being is for him always qualified by locutions of 'insofar as' or 'inasmuch as'. Indeed, in *Ethics IV* he seems to suggest that a completely free human being would have no understanding of good and evil. If human beings were 'born free', rather than attaining that condition only sparingly, they would 'form no concept of good and evil' (EIVP68). He hastens, though, to assure his readers that the hypothesis of being 'born free' is false. Being what they are – finite modes of God-or-Nature – human beings cannot be 'born free'.

In the *Ethics*, Spinoza rejects theories of good and evil that look to Nature for models of goodness or perfection. The political writings show just how radically this position reverses common ways of thinking of good and evil in relation to reason. Completely rational human beings would, according to Spinoza, endanger good governance. They would be incapable of forming those alliances, driven by shared vulnerabilities, which are the basis for the security – and the thriving – of all.

The final upshot of Spinoza's treatment of the relations between reason and the passions, across his major works, is confirmation of his key claims in *Ethics IV*: that human power is very limited, and infinitely surpassed by the power of external causes; that wisdom lies in recognising that human beings do not have an absolute power to adapt things outside them to their own use; that they are part of the whole of Nature, whose necessities they follow. Yet his philosophy also offers reassurance that human understanding, at its best, will be entirely satisfied with those limitations and will strive to persevere in that satisfaction.

The development of Spinoza's treatment of fear and hope throughout *Ethics IV*, and in his political writings, is an important thread in my attempts to bring his philosophy into contact with contemporary climate change debate. On the textual readings I have offered, Spinoza's full analyses of hope and fear carry an incipient recognition of the emotive force of futurity – of the sense of 'not yet'. In relation to hope, especially, Spinoza's analysis evokes an indeterminacy of outcome – of openness towards something ongoing, and as yet unresolved. That openness to the unknown permeates human efforts to persist, and to thrive, within a totality infinitely wider than themselves.

On my reading, Spinoza's full treatment of hope presents it as involving a tremulous anticipation of future joy – a yearning or longing, coloured by the possibility of nonfulfilment or loss, under the impact of rival forces. Fear, likewise, involves an agitated expectation of future sadness. In the fuller context of Spinoza's development of the collective and political dimensions of hope, in *Ethics IV* and in the political writings, that affectivity of the sense of the future becomes more salient.

Some of what Spinoza says in the *Ethics* about attitudes to the past and to the future can sound like an echo of Platonic preoccupation with the eternal; and some of it can sound like a Stoic aloofness from the emotional vicissitudes of temporal passage. Yet, on my reading, the upshot of his philosophy is very different from both.

It is important to keep in mind here that for Spinoza the distinctions between 'past', 'present' and 'future' are themselves constructs of imagination. Those constructs are caught up in imagination's structural interconnections with the affects – with desire and, more generally, with the strivings to persist associated with his concept of conatus.

Chantal Jaquet has argued that in Spinoza's philosophy those connections with emotion give tense distinctions an experiential fulness.[19] On her account, they are not for Spinoza merely subjective ways of ordering experience – to be set aside as irrelevant in the objective understanding of what is real. It is an analysis that perhaps lends some support to seeing Spinoza's treatment of hope as bearing more closely on contemporary emotional response to climate change than might have been expected from the Stoic echoes in some passages of the *Ethics*.

Putting it all together, I want to argue that Spinoza ends up in a place very different from Seneca's distrust and disdain of hope.

---

[19] Jaquet 2021.

There may, perhaps, be some playful irony in his suggesting, in the *Political Treatise*, that human beings who acted only from reason would make bad citizens. Yet, for him, entirely rational human beings are strange creatures of myth. Significantly, they are not heroes. That marks just how far he has moved from the ideals of a severe Stoicism.

'Loving-Kindness' and Humankind

The idealised friendships described by Spinoza in *Ethics IV*, and in his political writings, are relations between like-minded individuals, committed to pursuing – as far as humanly possible – the guidance of reason, in attaining release from the bondage of the passions. However the description of those friendships provides a model for wider relations of reciprocal loving-kindness that strengthen human collectivities.

Edwin Curley notes, in his translation of the *Theological-Political Treatise*, the difficulties in adequately translating the Latin terms in which Spinoza talks of that form of love which unites fellow human beings, intent on the cultivation of reason. Spinoza's articulation of the concept brings together aspects of *amor*, which can be directed from human beings towards God, and *caritas* – commonly construed as directed towards other human beings. In Spinoza's discussion in Chapters 13 and 14 of the *Theological-Political Treatise*, 'loving-kindness' also has biblical overtones – evoking the idea of a steadfast divine love, associated with justice.[20]

Spinoza's integration of reason, imagination and affect provides the basis for thinking of a dynamic form of fellow-feeling that strengthens human powers. While the term 'loving-kindness' resonates in more familiar concepts – compassion, sympathy and empathy – the fellow-feeling that Spinoza describes has some distinctive features.

Compassion, though its name suggests shared feelings, can be exercised without experiencing emotion – for example, as an aspect of public policy. Sympathy, which has a longer philosophical history, carries stronger connotations of shared emotion. Its

---

[20] Curley 2016: 641 (glossary entry: 'Love, Loving Kindness').

companion term 'empathy' is a more recent construct, functioning principally in ascriptions of a virtuous character trait. More recently, it has come to be used more generally, and vaguely, as a variant on 'respect' – as in locutions of 'empathy training' in response to workplace discrimination or harassment.

In contrast, loving-kindness is neither an emotional condition nor a purely intellectual state of understanding. It is not the pity that might be extended, from a position of assumed superiority, to a suffering 'other'. The term evokes a merging of affect and intellectual recognition. The 'loving' resides in affective acknowledgement of shared 'kind' – issuing in a reciprocal strengthening of powers.

I suggested earlier, in discussing Spinoza's attitude to the treatment of animals, that his analysis could permit the recognition of shared connection between human beings and other species – at any rate, where commonalities are recognised. The important point here is that such recognition of sameness or difference is not an abstract evaluation of how near a species might sit to 'human' in a classification system. Rather, it is an insight – imbued with affect – into affinities, yielding a desire for shared efforts to persist and thrive.

Thus understood, Spinozist 'loving-kindness' is a disposition cultivated through reason. Yet the term also captures the dynamic force for transformation which is for Spinoza inherent in human emotion. That accords with his insistence in *Ethics III* that it is not 'understanding', as such, that explains the power of a mind in relation to passions. The interconnection that yields loving-kindness emerges independently of rational deliberation.

On Spinoza's analysis, sympathetic connections between minds involve a kind of mimesis. 'If we imagine a thing like us, toward which we have had no affect, to be affected with some affect, we are thereby affected with a like affect' (EIIIP27). Yet this mimesis is more akin to a contagion of affect than to a studied imitation. In the course of his tabulated Definitions of the Affects, he makes it clear that, even in situations where 'imitation' seems applicable, it is not always to be construed as 'emulation'. Emulation, as Spinoza understands it, applies only where we imitate what we judge to be 'honourable, useful, or pleasant'.

If someone flees because he sees others flee, or is timid because he sees others timid, or, because he sees that someone else has burned his hand, withdraws his own hand and moves his body as if his hand were burned, we shall say that he imitates the other's affect, but not that he emulates it. (EIII Definitions of the Affects [after EIIIP59] Sec. XXXIII Exp.)

Despite its basis in unstudied imitation, Spinoza's version of sympathetic connection is not confined to the mere reverberation of the emotional state of a contiguous other. In keeping with his integrative view of reason, imagination and affect, this interaction of embodied minds involves understanding the other's emotional state, and a capacity to imagine oneself into their situation. This accords with his treatment of the dynamic interactions of imagination and affect, and with his insistence that their integration into reason must be understood, if human beings are not to live under the illusion of exemption from the necessities of Nature.

Spinoza's version of friendship as the model for loving-kindness is centred on a form of like-mindedness, grounded in his concept of conatus – the effort to persist in understanding, in which resides the essence of an individual mind. This form of friendship rests on apprehension of deep commonalities that bind human beings together, in contrast to the superficial conflicts and rivalries which drive them apart.

That aspiration may sound familiar in the context of contemporary political mantras of national unity. However the dynamism of Spinoza's version of conatus ensures that those commonalities are not construed merely in terms of individuals inertly falling under a shared definition. They involve an alignment of 'forces for existing', in which the strengths of each individual are reinforced and enhanced.

There are continuities here with a concept which Descartes, in his *Passions of the Soul*, called *générosité*. Though it may sound familiar, it is differently conceptualised from what is now commonly known as 'generosity'. In Descartes's definition, *générosité* is not associated with the benign distribution of goods, as in what might now be regarded as 'largesse'. Its connections are closer to the notion of a nature or *genus* held in common. The associations of generosity with benevolence, in more recent understanding of 'kindness', eclipse those connotations of 'kind'.

Descartes's *générosité* involves the recognition of shared qualities whose presence is cause for celebration, rather than envy. For those qualities are supposed 'also to be present, or at least capable of being present, in every other person'.[21] Similarly, for Spinoza, the recognition of commonalities is a source of joy. 'For insofar as each loves the same thing, each one's love is thereby encouraged, i.e. each one's Joy is thereby encouraged' (*EIVP34Schol.*). Like-mindedness between individual human beings yields joy in the recognition of affinities – and love in relation to the acknowledged cause of that joy.

Loving-kindness is the core of Spinoza's evocation in the *Ethics* of a noble form of friendship. His description echoes themes in ancient thought, including Aristotle's treatment of the friend as 'another self', in Chapter 8 of his *Nicomachean Ethics*. In Spinoza's version of that ideal, 'forces for existing', which reside in individual efforts to persist in being, are strengthened through collaborations with others – based on recognition of affinities in kind.

Friendship, thus understood, is a model for the broader consideration, in Spinoza's political writings, of relations of loving-kindness within human collectivities. His approach to political aspects of human interdependence is reflected in the *Ethics IV* account of the strengthening of human powers through friendship – an account grounded in his metaphysical concept of conatus. These connections give a distinctive twist to Spinoza's treatment of varying forms of political power.

It is not my concern here to engage in commentary on the strengths or weaknesses of Spinoza's political philosophy. However, there are some aspects of his treatment of power which highlight conceptual points that bear on contemporary climate change discourse.

---

[21] Descartes 1985: 384 (Part Three, Sec. 154).

Spinoza on Power and Essence

Spinoza's treatment of power in his political writings was largely shaped in response to the political philosophy of his contemporary Thomas Hobbes. Famously, Hobbes – especially in his early works – was sceptical about the political significance of the concrete power (*potentia*) residing in the agency of 'the people'. He argued that, on their emergence from the 'state of nature', the people concede that power to a sovereign – thus allowing the production of a different form of power (*potestas*), exerted not 'by' but 'on' them. With that ceding, the collective power of the people is 'dissolved'.

In a resonant remark in his *Elements of the Laws*, Hobbes observes:

> They say the people rebelleth, or the people demandeth, when it is no more than a dissolved multitude, of which though any one man may be said to demand or have a right to something, yet the heap, or multitude, cannot be said to demand or have any right to any thing.[22]

For Spinoza, in contrast, the concrete power of agency (*potentia*) is fostered and enhanced through reciprocal relations within human groups, and remains a force to be reckoned with by those in authority. As we have seen, Spinoza articulates that collective power in terms of the strengthening of individual force for existing, grounded in the dynamism of conatus, as expounded in the *Ethics*. Hence, he argues, that rulers need to be mindful, not just of the contagious spread of mindless passion in the multitude, but of more structured forms of collective *potentia*, which can threaten the vertical power relation of *potestas* which they exert on their subjects.[23]

---

[22] Thomas Hobbes, *Elements of the Laws*, II.2.11, as quoted in Field 2020b: 73.

[23] My account here of the relations between *potestas* and *potentia* and the contrasts between Spinoza and Hobbes on the power of 'the people' owes much to the excellent discussion of these issues in Field 2020b.

For Spinoza, the dynamics of human interconnection can yield social unities, within which the thriving of the one depends on, and can also enhance, that of others. 'The people' is thus for Spinoza capable of being much more than a Hobbesian 'dissolved multitude' or inchoate 'heap'.

Spinoza shares with Hobbes the view that the concept of 'right' is interdependent with that of 'power'. They also share rejection of the idea that free will marks a demarcation between human beings and other beings. There are also similarities in their treatment of human desire; Hobbes has his own version of the concept of conatus, as the urge driving persistence in being. However, Spinoza offers a much more fully developed treatment of the interactions between different 'strivings to persist', and of the possibilities thus created for the enhancement of human powers.

Here, Spinoza's treatment of the essence of a human mind offers insights that can be brought to bear on contemporary discussions of climate change. It offers an alternative to the notion of a pre-existing definable nature that demarcates humanity from the rest of the world. It may also help to soften sharp divisions between different 'peoples' within the totality of human beings.

In the context of climate change, appeal to notions of preexisting essence can blunt the recognition of commonalities across difference – both within and across species. Spinoza's dynamic notion of essence, in contrast, facilitates thinking of emergent affinities – commonalities which develop over time. On this way of thinking 'forces for existing' are strengthened in processes of reciprocal adaptation. It becomes possible to then envisage the development of further affinities across difference, in an indeterminate future. Emphasis on pre-existing essence, in contrast, facilitates orientation towards preservation of a determinate past.

Spinoza's version of essence, imbued with the striving inherent in conatus, evokes a dynamic interaction of powers – an enmeshing of strivings to persist. On this model, the recognition of powers and capacities shared with fellow humans continues to have special significance. Yet the open-ended character of essence, thus construed, allows for a less rigid marking of the differences between human and non-human. Humankind – and the reach of loving-

*kind*ness – need not then be construed in terms of predetermined properties, sharply demarcated from the rest of Nature.

Spinozist loving-*kind*ness may serve humans better than destructive illusions of supremacy over the non-human. I will argue in later chapters that it may provide a basis for rethinking unexamined assumptions at play in some specific issues under discussion in the context of climate change. Those possible applications will become clearer after considering *Ethics* V. There, we will see Spinoza offer a fuller treatment of the powers that human minds can exert within the necessities of Nature – through a form of affective understanding which lies beyond reason.

5

Beyond Reason

In the Preface to *Ethics* V, Spinoza returns to his preoccupation with what is wrong with Descartes's treatment of the human mind, focusing more directly now on the way it construes the role of reason in the management of emotion. He offers a scathing critique of Descartes's view of the mind as having absolute power over its passions through the exercise of a supposedly free human will. He cannot wonder enough, he says, that a philosopher of Descartes's apparent calibre should have made the preposterous claim that minds and bodies – such utterly different and distinct kinds of thing – should nonetheless causally interact.

Spinoza's own focus remains firmly on the human mind's embodiment within the necessities governing the totality of things. He promises that his alternative remedy for the passions will present the power of a mind as defined only by understanding, with no role for a specious free will. Once again, Spinoza puts a strong emphasis on the dynamics of the human mind's vacillations, and the steadying effects of reason. If affects can be separated from thoughts of an external cause, then – by his earlier arguments – 'the Love, or Hate, toward the external cause is destroyed, as are the vacillations of mind arising from these affects' (EVP2).

This has an initially surprising consequence: the power of the passions can, it seems, be overcome simply by better understanding them. 'An affect which is a passion ceases to be a passion as soon as we form a clear and distinct idea of it' (EVP3). Elaborating the point, Spinoza suggests that 'the more an affect is known to us, then, the more it is in our power, and the less the Mind is acted on by it' (EVP3Cor.). Hence 'each of us has – in part, at least, if not absolutely – the power to understand himself and his affects, and consequently, the power to bring it about that he is less acted on by them' (EVP4Schol.).

Reason's 'Remedy'

Better understanding human passions may well seem an implausible remedy for their destructive power. Theoretical understanding of the passions does not of itself seem likely to put a mind less under their sway. Clarifying the strategy, Spinoza emphasises that what is crucial is to detach the thought of the passion from its supposed cause. It then becomes apparent that achieving this separation does not come from a detached theoretical understanding. The strategy itself involves affect. The satisfaction that comes of adequate understanding allows the affect itself to be 'separated from the thought of an external cause and joined to true thoughts' (VP4Schol.).

It is important to remember at this point that for Spinoza the power of the affect of joy is inherent in human understanding, for he has defined joy in terms of a transition to greater mental activity. A mind's transition to active understanding is thus inherently joyful. Where a mind comes to greater understanding, the active force of the primary affect of joy is greater than the power of any passion. What is involved in Spinoza's 'remedy', then, is a deeply affective understanding, which he presents as the greatest possible power of the mind:

> We can devise no other remedy for the affects which depends on our power and is more excellent that this, which consists in a true knowledge of them. For the Mind has no other power than that of thinking and forming adequate ideas. (EVP4Schol.)

The consideration of time is again an important element in evaluating Spinoza's treatment of this intellectual power. As we have seen, especially in his treatment of hope and fear, the power of the passions is bound up – through their inter-relations with imagination – with the sense of past and future. Affects that arise from reason, in contrast, owe their power to their relation to the common properties of things, which are always regarded as present since 'there can be nothing which excludes their present existence' (EVP7Dem.). Those affects – if we 'take account of time' – are thus 'more powerful than those that are related to singular things which we regard as absent' (EVP7).

Spinoza's recurring reference to 'exclusion from existence' is significant here, echoing his earlier talk of the power of images to exclude one another, and also his analysis of freedom in terms of absence of 'external' determination. Drawing those themes together, Spinoza now presents the power of reason over the passions as operating through its capacity to focus the mind on its joyful satisfaction with what is present to it.

On Spinoza's account, engagement with things present disrupts the allure of future pleasure. It also breaks mental fixation on the loss of things past. Yet there is surely something lacking in this happy picture of a mind satisfied in its apprehension of 'the common properties of things'. Individuality slipped through the net of understanding in Spinoza's treatment of the distinction between imagination and reason – his 'first' and 'second' kinds of knowledge. Now, it seems, the mind's joyful satisfaction in what is delivered through reason also comes at the cost of a disengagement from – and lack of regard for – 'singular things'.

Intuitive Knowledge and Singularity

The story, however, does not end with reason's disengagement from singularity. The mind – elated though it may be at the apprehension of generalities through reason – has within it a striving to reach a yet higher kind of knowledge. It aspires to what Spinoza calls 'intuitive knowledge'.

Readers attuned to a familiar philosophical progression, dramatised in Plato's *Dialogues* – from the understanding of particulars to apprehension of abstract universal 'forms' – may be surprised here to find that Spinoza's highest kind of knowledge seems to move towards a different goal. It involves reaching beyond reason's concern with universals in a way that yields access to singularity, without loss of 'adequacy'.

For Spinoza, this shift from universals to particulars is a progression rather than a regression. On his treatment of human knowledge, reason of itself does not access particulars; and the lower kinds of knowledge yield only 'inadequate' knowledge of them. Finally, with his account of the highest kind of knowledge, adequate understanding can come together with access to singularity.

In relation to Spinoza's 'remedy' for the debilitating effects of passions, reason shares the power of intuitive knowledge. It has the capacity to school the imagination, so that a mind's love or hate is detached from the idea of an 'external' cause of joy or sorrow. The mind then focuses instead on its own joy in actively understanding – a satisfaction that is not dependent on what lies outside its own power. The more a mind engages in that shift of focus, the more will its own powers be strengthened.

Here again, Spinoza's recommended strategy of detachment and reattachment may sound like an esoteric exercise in mental gymnastics. Yet he is at pains to point out that this schooling of the imagination is framed by his recurring locutions of 'for the most part' or 'insofar as'. Moreover, the joyful – though demanding – exercise of reason has its less arduous ancillary support in the cultivation of sensible strategies of imagination, grounded in everyday life experience.

Spinoza, however, goes on to present reason as straining beyond its own powers – as well as appropriating to its own use the more familiar resources of imagination. 'The Mind can bring it about that all the Body's affections, or images of things, are related to the idea of God' (*EVP*14). While being true of all the body's affections, that does not mean that the exercise can be performed for all of them, all the time. Unspoken locutions of 'insofar as' and 'for the most part' continue to hover. In the accompanying demonstration, Spinoza offers a reformulation: 'There is no affection of the Body of which the Mind cannot form some clear and distinct concept', and hence bring it about that 'they are related to the idea of God' (*EVP*14Dem.).

The referral of 'affections or images' to the idea of God marks the shift to Spinoza's highest form of knowledge. It lies beyond the reach of what imagination can contribute; for it arises from reason's access to adequate ideas. However, understanding this transition brings also a new way of thinking of the mind's powers of thought. Spinoza is describing a kind of thinking that involves, not a descent to the lower kinds of knowledge, but rather a capacity for the intuitive understanding that lies beyond reason.

Knowing in Relation to the Idea of God

What exactly is the content of this referral of the body's affections to the idea of God? Spinoza takes himself to have already demonstrated, in *Ethics IV*, that the idea of God is itself readily accessible to all, though it is also often misconstrued. The adequate idea of God is for him not an abstruse notion, accessible only to a select few rarified thinkers. It is inherent in the conatus of a human mind.

To have this readily available understanding of God it is not necessary to advance to Spinoza's highest kind of knowledge. What does require intuitive knowing, however, is the understanding of an individual thing in relation to the idea of God. In intuitive understanding, a mind can come to apprehend an actually existing thing in its dependence on God-or-substance.

A striking feature of Spinoza's argumentative strategy here is that it relies on affective aspects of the idea of God. This idea, like other ideas, is an act of the mind – a transition to greater activity. It is, by definition, joyful; and – from previous arguments – it is 'adequate'. 'The idea of God which is in us is adequate and perfect. So insofar as we consider God, we act. Consequently there can be no Sadness accompanied by the idea of God' (EVP18Dem.).

Intuitive knowledge is joy in the idea of God. Hence, by his previous definitions of affects, it is also love of God. That affective understanding of things in relation to God delivers the fullness of the power of an active human mind within Nature.

The inter-relations of reason, imagination and affect remain constantly in view throughout *Ethics V*. However, the argumentative strategy demands those locutions of 'insofar as' or 'inasmuch as', to which Spinoza has so often resorted. Even at the height of its power, a human mind remains embedded in the totality of finite things. Hence, it remains always susceptible to the fluctuating powers of other modes within the wholeness of Nature.

In *Ethics* V, there is an additional layer to Spinoza's use of the 'insofar as' locution, through which he refines his articulation of intuitive knowledge as affective understanding – a mind's intellectual love of God. This love, he says, is 'the most constant of all the affects'. For 'insofar as it is related to the Body, [it]cannot be destroyed, unless it is destroyed with the Body itself' (EVP20Schol.). He promises to deal later with what this intellectual love of God is, 'insofar as it is related only to the Mind'. The terrain for that final articulation has been demarcated in advance. It is in delivering on the promise – in the concluding sections of the *Ethics* – that he intends to deliver the full story of the power of a human mind.

The recurring locutions of 'insofar as' or 'in as much as' serve as reminders that the whole discussion is framed by Spinoza's insistent construal of the human mind within the context of its embodiment within the whole of Nature. *Ethics* IV addressed the power of the mind, insofar as that power is vulnerable to being acted upon by other forces within Nature. Propositions 1–20 of *Ethics* V have addressed the power of the mind insofar it acts within Nature in accordance with its own power, epitomised in the capacity for adequate understanding through reason. The concluding sections of *Ethics* V now address that active power of the mind, insofar as it relates to the mind alone. Throughout all those qualifications, the totality of Nature remains in the picture. Yet it is only in the final sections of the *Ethics* that the contrast term to 'totality' – the mind's own individuality – comes to the foreground.

Individuality comes back into the story with the mind's power to understand itself in relation to the idea of substance, on which the totality depends. Much of Spinoza's argumentation hinges on consideration of the particular idea that is the mind itself. However, this consideration brings with it the subsidiary ideas of finite things which are included within the idea that is the mind.

Embodiment, Mortality and Eternity

Spinoza's emphasis on the embodiment of the human mind now takes a different turn. Since embodiment is inherent in the very being of a human mind, there is no possibility of it continuing to exist after bodily death. As the idea of an actually existing body, 'the Mind can neither imagine anything, nor recollect past things except while the Body endures' (EVP21Dem.).

Spinoza's rejection of any form of embodiment after death need not be taken as suggesting that a human mind might nonetheless continue to exist, without being able to either imagine or remember. He insists that duration itself – continued existence through time – has no application to a mind, beyond bodily existence:

> We do not attribute to the human Mind any duration that can be defined by time, except insofar as it expresses the actual existence of the Body, which is explained by duration, and can be defined by time, i.e. we do not attribute duration to it except while the Body endures. (EVP23Dem.)

Spinoza nonetheless goes on immediately to insist – in some of the most moving and eloquent language of the *Ethics* – that 'we feel and know by experience that we are eternal'. Elaborating that ultimate articulation of the content of his highest kind of knowledge, he adds: 'For the eyes of the mind, by which it sees and observes things, are the demonstrations themselves' (EVP23Schol.).

It is language profoundly fitting for the articulation of a philosophy that affirms the inter-relations of reason, imagination and emotion. The concept of imagining was associated, in *Ethics II*, with the inadequacy of felt awareness of body. It now re-enters, at the end of *Ethics V*, to forge a close relationship between 'feeling and knowing by experience' and the mind's exercise of its highest form of knowing – beyond reason.

Spinoza's talk of 'eyes of the mind' is of course metaphorical; such talk is itself an exercise of imagination. Yet in these final passages of the *Ethics*, his writing evokes an alliance between the exercise of a kind of imagining and reason. The relationship becomes clearer in a later passage, where he talks explicitly of a way of thinking 'as if'. The language evokes a construction of philosophical fictions, which act as sophisticated ancillaries to the insights of deductive reason:

> Although we are already certain that the Mind is eternal, insofar as it conceives things under a species of eternity, nevertheless,

for an easier explanation and better understanding of the things we wish to show, we shall consider it as if it were now beginning to be, and were beginning to understand things under a species of eternity, as we have done up to this point. We may do this without danger of error provided we are careful to draw our conclusions only from evident premises. (EVP31Schol.)

Having denied that the mind has duration – except while the body endures – it is, strictly, a fiction to think of its intuitive self-understanding as 'beginning to be'. Yet Spinoza's 'eyes of the mind' can, it seems, be trusted not to let their 'demonstrations' run beyond the rigorous demands of reason. However eloquent and moving these evocative interplays of imagination, deductive reason and philosophical fictions may be, there remains the challenge of giving some clear content to the nuances of Spinoza's talk of the mind's construing itself as eternal.

Knowing Oneself as Eternal

On my reading of these final sections of the *Ethics*, Spinoza's talk of the mind as eternal is not to be taken as claiming that it continues to exist after death, in some transformed state – whether of enhancement or of deprivation. Within the frame of Spinoza's insistence on embodiment, his talk of the mind recognising its own eternity suggests a way in which a mind can come to think of itself while it still exists. Spinoza enacts that way of thinking in the exhilarating, though challenging, final passages of the *Ethics*.

However, it must be acknowledged that the opinion of commentators on these passages is divided. Some interpret Spinoza as offering a theory of the partial survival of the mind beyond death, without memory or imagination. Spinoza does indeed say: 'The human Mind cannot be absolutely destroyed with the Body, but something of it remains which it is eternal' (EVP23). In the demonstration of that proposition, he returns to the language of 'essences', which he used in *Ethics II*, in discussing ideas in the mind of God. 'In God there is necessarily a concept, or idea, which expresses the essence of the human Body, an idea, therefore, which is necessarily something that pertains to the essence of the human Mind' (*EVP23Dem.*).

That talk of essences may well seem to open the possibility of a mind persisting beyond death – though as an 'essence', rather than as an actually existing thing. In a scholium, Spinoza adds the tantalising comment to which I referred earlier:

> Though it is impossible that we should recollect that we existed before the Body – since there cannot be any traces of this in the body, and eternity can neither be defined by time nor have any relation to time – still, we feel and know by experience that we are eternal. (*EVP23Schol.*)

Some commentators have read that sentence as indeed suggesting a kind of non-durational existence beyond death. Others – perhaps less patient – have dismissed these final passages in the *Ethics* as a retreat to incoherent mysticism. Edwin Curley – without either endorsing or dismissing the construal of Spinoza's 'eternity of the mind' as a version of survival beyond death – sums up the interpretive dilemma in a footnote to his translation of that notorious scholium:

> This sentence illustrates well the kind of difficulty characteristic of this part of the *Ethics*. On the face of it, Spinoza implies that we (who are here identified with parts of our minds; cf. IIP13C) not only will exist *after* the body, but did exist *before* it (though he denies the Platonic doctrine that we can come to recollect our pre-existence). But in the same breath he asserts that we are eternal (cf. IIA1 and ID8) and that the eternal has no relation to time.[1]

In that same scholium, Spinoza adds:

> [W]e feel that our mind, insofar as it involves the essence of the body under a species of eternity, is eternal, and that this existence it has cannot be defined by time or explained through

[1] Curley 1985: 608.

duration. Our mind, therefore, can be said to endure, and its existence can be defined by a certain time, only insofar as it involves the actual existence of the body . . . (EVP23Schol.)

I want to suggest that those memorable – though not readily intelligible – sentences do not have to be interpreted as saying that anything of a human mind exists beyond the death of the body of which it is the idea. Spinoza's point is that a mind's being eternal is not to be thought of in terms of time at all. On my interpretation, he should not be taken as postulating a way of being that somehow transcends the durational existence of finite things. He is talking of a way of construing an actually existing thing.

Spinoza's point is that a human mind can – while it actually exists – come to understand itself in a way that prescinds from its actual existence. Derivatively, it can also apprehend, in that way, the ideas which are included within its own being – ideas retained from the impact of other bodies on its own. This understanding is not the apprehension of a distinctive property or character possessed by a human mind, which somehow makes it eternal. It is a distinctive way in which a mind can, while living, come to apprehend itself and the ideas it encompasses.

This 'intuitive' understanding is attained by a mind while its body actually exists – and hence, of course, while that mind itself actually exists. It involves grasping the truth of its own 'essence' being included in what Spinoza calls 'the mind of God' – substance, totally expressed under the attribute of thought. This insight in no way negates Spinoza's claim that the mind's actual existence – which is 'durational' – depends on its continued embodiment within the totality of finite modes of thought. Nor should the inclusion of its essence in the mind of God be construed as a special kind of being that somehow transcends duration.

As Spinoza has all along insisted, for a human mind, the only possible kind of existence involves embodiment within the totality of other finite modes. That actual existence is mediated through the totality. Yet, in intuitive understanding, the mind's focus is on a vertical axis of dependence. It comes to grasp the fullness of its status as a mode of God-as-substance, while yet being aware also that its actual existence is mediated through the horizontal axis of dependence – through the totality of which it is part.

Joy and Fear of Death

There remains room for disagreement about the exact content of Spinoza's version of the eternity of the mind. However, it is clear that the power he attributes to intuitive understanding arises from its involving the affective force of joy. It is joy, as transition to greater mental activity, that gives this highest kind of knowledge its power to overcome the force of other finite things, which can put the mind into states of sadness and 'bondage'.

Affect is inherent in this understanding, rather than an add-on. As an exercise of the mind's greatest power, within the totality of Nature, this way of knowing brings 'the greatest Joy' and 'the greatest satisfaction' (*EVP27Dem.*). The tone in these passages may suggest affinities with religious experience. Joyous love of God seems to be presented as the portal through which a finite mind enters on Spinoza's version of the apprehension of the eternal. Yet this affective understanding is directed not towards a transcendent being, but towards finite individual things encompassed in the totality of finite modes. In elaborating its nature, Spinoza emphasises the understanding of singular things: 'The more we understand singular things, the more we understand God' (*EVP24*).

The central point here rests on the definitions of Spinoza's metaphysics, which he presented in *Ethics I*. The final outcome, at the end of *Ethics V*, is a greater depth of understanding of the basic truth enunciated in those opening definitions: particular things are nothing but finite modes of substance, expressed under an attribute. What may have seemed, at the beginning, an arid abstract articulation of the metaphysics of substance and modes has, at the end, become an emotionally charged understanding of human finitude. Spinoza has presented the mind's apprehension of itself as eternal as implicit in its recognition of its own inherent dependence on substance – on God-or-Nature.

Echoing old Stoic themes, Spinoza relates the joy that comes from intuitive understanding to a shift of attachment away from changeable things. Those things, he says, are susceptible to many variations, so that we are never able to fully possess them. In the final sections of the *Ethics*, a mind shifts attention away from the duration of things, focusing instead on their status as modifications of God-or-Nature. That shift, 'begets a Love toward a thing immutable and eternal, which we really fully possess' (*EVP20Schol.*).

Spinoza presents that shift of attention as yielding a joy that can overcome the fear of death. The language may resonate with an austere Stoicism. Yet this remaking of ancient ideals of detachment involves neither a severe distrust of affects nor a flight of reason to Platonic universals. The orientation of Spinoza's 'intellectual love of God' is towards singular things. That gives it a greater power than reason's apprehension of universals.

> For although I have shown generally in Part I that all things (and consequently the human Mind also) depend on God both for their essence and their existence, nevertheless, that demonstration, though legitimate and put beyond all chance of doubt, still does not affect our Mind as much as when this is inferred from the very essence of any singular thing which we say depends on God. (*EVP36Schol.*)

The apprehension of things under the species of eternity is already available to the mind through reason's grasp of unvarying 'essences'. What makes intuitive understanding distinctive is the ability to apprehend, through that lens of eternity, things in their particularity – changeable things, which begin and cease to exist. Applied to the essence of its own body, of which it is the idea, this shift of focus is a profound transition – a more powerful way of apprehending its own existence than is available to it through either of the lower kinds of knowing.

In intuitive understanding, the mind is able to apprehend its own existence in a way that prescinds from its continued existence in time. Yet this is not an apprehension that sets it apart from the body of which it is the idea. 'This power of conceiving things under a species of eternity pertains to the Mind only insofar as it conceives the Body's essence under a species of eternity' (*EVP29Dem.*).

The transition to intuitive understanding involves a mind coming to see itself as idea of an actually existing body, whose essence is included within the totality of all the modes of God-or-Nature. Yet the objects of such apprehension are not abstract universals. 'To conceive things under a species of eternity is . . . to conceive things insofar as they are conceived through God's essence, as real beings, or insofar as through God's essence they involve existence' (EVP30Dem.).

It is complex argumentation – and the shifts between different philosophical notions of 'essence' are dense. Yet the upshot of these final sections of the *Ethics* yields a rich content for Spinoza's equation of intuitive understanding with a joyous intellectual love of God-or-Nature. In another exercise of the locution of 'insofar as' or 'inasmuch as', he says that this joy or love of God arises 'not insofar as we *imagine* him as present, but insofar as we *understand* God to be eternal' (EVP32Cor.; my emphasis).

It is striking here that, although Spinoza is dealing with a form of knowledge that he presents as higher than reason, he continues to emphasise the shift from misleading ways of imagining God to a corrected way of understanding God-or-Nature. Reason continues to monitor imagining, even when intuitive knowing has moved beyond the power of reason.

At the end of the *Ethics* – as at its beginning – the God invoked is no ordinary God; and Spinoza is bound by no theological orthodoxies, which might restrain the conclusions he reaches about it. Nor does he hesitate to resort to his own philosophical fictions in describing a human mind's relations to such a God. Strictly speaking, Spinoza's God has no affects – not even divine ones. It has no love for human beings – or even for itself. Its perfection rules out the transitions in activity in terms of which Spinoza defines the affects. Yet a reasoned philosophical fiction is not a fantasy.

Guided by his own insistence that deductions – as the 'eyes of the Mind' – must observe logical rigour, Spinoza proceeds to reason his way through the nuances of his 'intellectual love of God' – again with a sprinkling of 'insofar as' locutions. He argues that a mind's intellectual love of such a God as this must be 'the very love of God by which God loves himself'. However, this love is directed to God 'not insofar as he is infinite, but insofar as he can be explained by the human Mind's essence, considered under a species of eternity' (*EVP36*). Hence, 'God's love of men and the Mind's intellectual Love of God are one and the same' (*EVP36Cor.*).

The Love of God-or-Nature

Spinoza's equation of human beings' love of God with God's love of them may seem a preposterous play on the ambiguity in 'the love of God' – as 'God's love' or as 'love directed towards God'. A finite human mind – a speck within an infinite totality – is here presented as claiming participation in the divine nature. Yet this has been all along implicit in Spinoza's metaphysics of substance and modes. The being of this God, after all, incorporates in its modes all that exists – including human minds, their affections and affects. 'Our Mind, with respect both to essence and existence, follows from the divine nature, and continually depends on God' (*EVP36Schol.*).

Seeing the logical progression in Spinoza's reasoning is one thing. Fully grasping the integration of understanding, imagination and affect enacted in that reasoning process may be even more demanding. Yet the emotive force of the argumentation can bring a shock of recognition – as if the 'eyes of the mind' have opened to the full realisation of the nature of human thought processes as themselves fully modes of God-or-Nature, embedded within that totality.

The final argumentative move – into a mind's recognition of itself as 'eternal' – may for many readers remain a step too far. Through Spinoza's highest form of knowing, a human mind is supposed to gain insight into its own participation in the mind of God. It is also supposed to reach the fullest apprehension of itself as located inexorably within the whole of Nature. On Spinoza's view of God, those two notions ultimately come to one and the same thing. However, for contemporary readers, while talk of the 'whole of Nature' strikes a familiar chord, talk of a non-transcendent 'mind of God' remains more opaque.

Spinoza's response to that anticipated incredulity is in keeping with a strategy he has pursued throughout the entire *Ethics*.

He seeks to ease the reader out of a fixity of imagination, which blocks the recognition of something that is in fact already known:

> If we attend to the common opinion of men, we shall see that they are indeed conscious of the eternity of their Mind, but that they confuse it with duration, and attribute it to the imagination, or memory, which they believe remains after death. (*EVP34Schol.*)

Earlier, Spinoza claimed that the 'common opinion of men' already has – without their realising it – an adequate understanding of the nature of God. That adequate understanding is masked. For 'common opinion' confuses the ability to understand the nature of God with the ability to imagine it. He now suggests that a similar fixation with imagery is at play in how human minds typically construe the notion of themselves as 'eternal'. They confuse it with the notion of their existing forever.

The prospect of an existence beyond death in which there is no possibility of remembering or imagining anything may well seem, in any case, to be an unappealing content to being eternal. Would it be existence as a mind at all? However, Spinoza's point is that such a way of thinking of being eternal rests on a misconstrual of what it is to understand oneself as eternal – a resort to imagining, in the lack of understanding.

Strange though it might initially seem, being mortal and being eternal are, for Spinoza, not contradictory; they do not cancel one another out. They are different ways of apprehending the being of singular things in relation to the whole of which they are part. On Spinoza's account, imagining continued existence beyond death, is a spurious remedy for the fear of death. What can remove that fear is a mind's active, inherently joyful, exercise of its own power – fully present within the world in which, as yet, it actually exists.

At the end of the *Ethics*, Spinoza insists – as he has in its earlier parts – that the power of a human mind resides in understanding. The highest achievement of that understanding is one and the same with what he calls the 'intellectual love of God' – the affective understanding of one's own inclusion in the totality of being. He concludes that nothing can destroy that love; for there is nothing that has a power contrary to it. 'If there were something contrary to this Love, it would be contrary to the true; consequently, what could remove this Love would bring it about that what is true would be false. This (as is known through itself) is absurd' (EVP37Dem.).

It remains true – as Spinoza stated in the first axiom of *Ethics IV* – that there is no singular thing in nature than which there is not another more powerful and stronger. Yet that truth, he now explains, concerns 'singular things insofar as they are considered in relation to a certain time and place' (EVP37Schol.). The two ways of considering a singular thing – in relation to 'duration' and in relation to 'eternity' – coexist; they do not involve an impossible conjunction of logical opposites. They coexist through the integration of reason and intuitive knowledge in a mind's act of understanding its own status as a mode of substance.

Spinoza's 'intellectual love of God' does not make a human mind immortal. What it can offer is release – while the mind does exist – from fear of its own inevitable end. However, here – yet again – Spinoza's conclusions are framed by locutions of 'in so far as' or 'in as much as'.

To describe the intellectual love of God as unable to be destroyed is not to say that it is possible for a human being to live always in that state. For human minds are inexorably embodied within the whole of Nature – living in continuous flux, and ever changing for better and worse. Yet, within the frame of those inevitable fluctuations of human power within the totality of modes, there remains the possibility of finding the deep satisfaction that comes from understanding ever better their presence in the world. What is found so rarely, Spinoza concludes, must be hard. 'But all things excellent are as difficult as they are rare' (EVP42Schol.).

In all of this, Spinoza is talking of mortality in a context where he did not have to contemplate catastrophic extinctions – including perhaps that of his own species. Yet something of what he has to say about fear of death does carry over into the consideration of climate change grief. There may be increasingly little scope for optimism. Yet, out of the immediacy of grief at all that is lost – human and non-human – the effort to better understand human presence in Nature may yet bring some hope of salvaging a shared future.

6
Alternative Interpretations

In previous chapters, I have offered a reading of the *Ethics* that tracks the structure of the work, while highlighting points at which its central theses and argumentation can be brought into engagement with contemporary climate change issues. That attempted application of Spinoza's philosophy rests on two inter-related claims about the text, both of which emphasise the centrality of Spinoza's critique of Descartes.

The first claim is that Spinoza's treatment of human thought throughout the *Ethics* offers a model of its inclusion within the natural world, repudiating the Cartesian model of separation. The second is that Spinoza articulates a structural integration within the human mind of reason, imagination and emotion – a view that runs counter to a common interpretation of him as a 'rationalist'. Those two claims enable an application of the text to contemporary challenges in rethinking human presence in Nature in the context of climate change.

I have presented Spinoza's philosophy as having the potential to assist in reconceptualising common assumptions about human supremacy within the natural world. However, it must be acknowledged that the interpretations on which I have rested that application are not themselves uncontested. I wish, in this chapter, to address some of those issues of textual interpretation.

There can be no denying that, along with the many passages I have quoted from the *Ethics* in support of my reading of Spinoza's version of reason, there are others that seem to pull in another direction. Reason may be ubiquitous in the text; but it also seems to have a shifting position in relation to the totality of being.

Locating Reason

Where, exactly, according to Spinoza, is reason? It may seem a strange question. Yet it has been found sufficiently intelligible to admit of differing answers. One common interpretation is that for Spinoza, reason resides in the order of the universe – that he regards it as manifested in the structure of the world, which human minds seek to understand. On that way of thinking, reason has a status independent of human minds; it is inherent in the ordered structure of reality – whether or not that order is adequately perceived by human beings. On an alternative interpretation, which fits more neatly with my reading, Spinoza treats reason as belonging within human minds, holding a limited position – as those minds themselves do – within the whole.

The notion of reason as residing in the order of the universe seems to be supported by Spinoza's references, especially in *Ethics II*, to a perfect correspondence between an 'order of thought' and an 'order of things'. Such talk evokes an alignment on a grand scale between thought and the material world. It is not surprising, then, that Spinoza is often taken to have offered a bold articulation of what may well be considered the ultimate 'rationalist' dream: a perfect match in which human reasoning mirrors the order of the whole of Nature.

That picture of an alignment of human thought with rationally ordered Nature may seem to be antithetical to the central theme that I have been concerned to track through the *Ethics*: that human thought is itself inextricably immersed within Nature, and has therefore only a limited perspective from within the totality of being. That location of reason seems to accord, especially, with passages I have discussed from *Ethics IV*, where Spinoza offers an account of the limitations of human powers of thought within Nature. Its upshot is perhaps most succinctly expressed in his tantalising observation in Chapter 16 of the *Theological-Political Treatise* about the insignificance of the laws of human reason within the whole of Nature. He says there:

Nature is not constrained by the laws of human reason, which aim only at man's true advantage and preservation. It is governed by infinite other laws, which look to the eternal order of the whole of nature of which man is only a small part. It is only by the necessity of this order that all individuals are determined to exist and have effects in a definite way.[1]

The two pictures of reason's relations with Nature seem to involve radically different ways of positioning reason. Can Spinoza consistently evoke both? Whatever strangeness they encounter in Spinoza's talk of the 'mind of God', contemporary readers can readily take from the *Ethics* the insight that human thought itself – not just the objects of that thought – is included within the totality of finite things. On the other hand, there is that grand articulation of the correspondence between the totality of thought and the totality of things, which seems to postulate an outside view on two aligned totalities.

On one interpretation, reason seems to govern the whole of Nature. On the other, thought is itself included under the necessities which bind the whole. On the one model, a human mind mirrors the order of Nature. On the other, a human mind is a confused confluence of processes within a totality it cannot hope to encompass; and reason itself is a mere speck within that whole. Reading the *Ethics* can seem to demand shifting constantly between those different ways of positioning reason.

In trying to make sense of Spinoza's treatment of reason, it comes easily to imagine one's own thinking as outside what he talks of as the totality of ideas, at an external standpoint. That, after all, is the natural position from which to understand and evaluate a philosophical text. One situates oneself outside the text of the *Ethics*, as one considers the array of propositions, definitions, proofs and ancillary apparatus. Yet, if this text is true, there is ultimately no such position at which a human mind can position itself in relation to its world. From where is a human mind, regarded by Spinoza as a finite mode of thought, supposed to contemplate the separate orders of mind and of matter – of 'thought' and of 'things'?

[1] Curley 2016: 284.

These tensions do not reside only in a text written by Spinoza in the seventeenth century, to be resolved through a current contest of interpretations. Something of the same ambiguity lies at the heart of the contemporary challenge of adequately articulating the conceptual dilemmas posed by understanding human presence in the 'natural' world. Both ways of thinking continue to be at play in climate change discourse – mostly without any clear articulation of the implications of either. Their interplay in the *Ethics* can help illuminate some of those tensions within contemporary attitudes to human presence in Nature – even if there is no definitive answer to the question which textual interpretation is the correct one.

Reason and Necessity

The philosophical issues at stake in the positioning of human thought in relation to Nature – as those issues have come to be understood in contemporary thought – were articulated by Immanuel Kant in the eighteenth century. In Kant's famous formulation of the relations between thought and reality, the conceptual categories operating within human thought are the conditions under which the world becomes intelligible. Those categories do not reveal the natures of things as they really are; they are the necessary conditions under which that reality appears to human understanding.

Inevitably, to read Spinoza now is, to some extent, to see his treatment of reason through the lens of the Kantian treatment of human knowing – no less than his treatment of Nature is now seen through the lens of post-Kantian idealism and Romanticism. Against that Kantian background, Spinoza's version of reason seems to shift between two positions that can now be seen more clearly as different: as a feature of mind-independent reality; or as an aspect of human minds, having no bearing on how the world really is. The reading I have offered of Spinoza highlights the latter strand throughout Spinoza's philosophy. Yet it must be acknowledged that the other strand is also present; and that – at some points in the texts – it may well seem the more plausible reading.

My own preferred response to the tensions in Spinoza's treatment of reason is to hold firmly to his central thesis of embodied human thought, according to which a mind strives – within the totality of finite modes – to understand itself, God and other things. Within that frame of embodiment within the totality, a mind exercises its powers – insofar as it can do so – for ever more adequate understanding. That effort involves the cultivation and exercise of reason. However, given Spinoza's emphasis on the interconnections between reason, imagination and affect, a mind's striving to better understand is not an exercise of reason alone. Indeed, his treatment of intuitive understanding provides a model for rigorous philosophical imagination, in which the mind can allow itself to think 'as if' its understanding reaches above or beyond the totality in which it is immersed.

It is in the enactment, in the final sections of the *Ethics*, of philosophical imagination – imbued with affect – that the inadequacy of the categorisation of Spinoza as a 'rationalist' emerges most clearly. He does treat the cultivation of reason as a superior source of theoretical knowledge – higher than sensory experience, raw images or memory. In that respect, he can be seen as a committed 'rationalist'. Yet the invocation of that familiar – though increasingly outmoded – categorisation of kinds and styles of philosophy does not do his thinking justice. It yields an impoverished picture of his nuanced treatment of the life of the mind, which unfolds in the *Ethics* as a whole.

At the very least, Spinoza offers a transformed version of reason, which resists the assumption of its supremacy – either within a human mind or with regard to the positioning of human beings within the rest of Nature. His conjunction of the celebration of reason with an insistence on its limitations within Nature is one of the things that can make reading him now relevant to challenges in understanding human presence within a changing planet.

Thought, Things and Expression

Commentators who see Spinoza as an archetype of 'rationalism' tend to downplay his insistence that human thought is itself immersed within the totality of being, stressing instead his affirmation of the complete correspondence between the order of thought and the order of things. Since my own reading lays the stress on themes of human embodiment and illusion in totality, it is appropriate to consider what then can be made of Spinoza's talk of that overarching alignment of 'orders' of 'thought' and of 'things'.

The content to be given to that grand picture depends on the interpretation, in turn, of the crucial concept of expression, through which Spinoza affirms the correspondence of the two 'orders'. It is an evocative notion of unity amid difference, which interpreters have struggled to elucidate. 'Expression' has made sporadic appearances throughout the history of philosophy, without having a clear trajectory within it. Let us look more closely at what we have already seen of how Spinoza uses it.

God-or-substance is, in Spinoza's terminology, completely 'expressed' both as extension and as thought. Under the attribute of extension that 'expression' yields a totality of finite material things. Under the attribute of thought, it yields a totality of finite modes of thought – ideas. Because each totality expresses the whole being of substance, there is nothing expressed under the one attribute that is not also expressed under the other. Thus, something cannot figure on one side of the division of 'orders' without a correlate on the other side. Hence, Spinoza argues, there can be no causal relations between the two totalities.

For Spinoza, causal relations hold only within – not across – attributes. What exists on one side of the thought–extension distinction is causally independent of what exists on the other side. Minds and bodies are nonetheless related across that divide – as ideas to their objects.

In trying to make sense of Spinoza's version of the relation between thought and its objects, it comes readily to think of this notion of 'expression' in terms of a parallelism between two separate series of items – finite 'ideas' and finite material things. Cast in terms of Spinoza's metaphysical categories, that will then be two series of finite modes – correlated, but never coming together.

'Parallelism' is not a concept that Spinoza himself used to describe the relationship between minds and bodies. However, it was used by Leibniz – to describe a relationship that was in some respects similar, though within a very different metaphysical system. Leibniz employed it in describing the inter-related content of a multiplicity of individual substances – in his term monads – that mirror in their internal complexity their interconnection.

Individual minds are for Spinoza not substances, but modes of the one unique substance; whereas for Leibniz – in this respect, like Descartes – there is a multiplicity of individual substances, some of which are minds. Yet there are resonances, in Leibniz's account of monads, of Spinoza's use of the concept of expression to describe the relations between minds and bodies. Within Leibniz's system, there is a parallelism between the internal content of individual mind-substances. They can be imagined as mapped, one onto another.

Chantal Jaquet, in her study of Spinoza's treatment of the affects, has called attention – in her account of Spinoza's views on the relations between what happens in human minds and in human bodies – to Leibniz's use of parallelism. However, she argues that the nuances of Spinoza's use of the concept of expression are at odds with the analogy of non-converging parallel lines.[2]

Jaquet was responding to the treatment of parallelism in Gilles Deleuze's extensive study *Expressionism in Philosophy: Spinoza*, in which he explored the affinities – and the contrasts – between Spinoza's use of 'expression' and a range of the term's other philosophical appearances. While acknowledging that Spinoza does not himself use the analogy with parallel lines, Deleuze suggested that the comparison nonetheless serves to capture something of the elusive noncausal interconnection of Spinoza's modes under different attributes.

On Jaquet's analysis, the analogy with parallel lines inappropriately emphasises difference – rather than unity – in giving content to Spinoza's talk of the expression of substance. She argues that Deleuze's cautious endorsement of the parallelism analogy serves, in its own way, to reduce unity to uniformity. On her own account, Spinoza has not superimposed mind and matter on one another in any way that answers to the image of parallel lines. Their unity, she suggests, is better construed through highlighting

[2] Jaquet 2018: 12–19.

Spinoza's own term 'equality' – with connotations of being 'the same' or 'at one'.

Jacquet's critique of the parallel lines analogy is directed to the interpretation of Spinoza's approach to the unity of individual minds and bodies – to the understanding of human affects – rather than to the inter-relations of the attributes of substance. Yet it does open up possibilities for alternative ways of thinking of expression that might better capture Spinoza's version of the relation between the 'orders' of 'thought' and of 'things'. Her suggested alternative rendering of Spinoza's talk of expression highlights his emphasis on themes associated with dynamic power – as in the notion of force for existing, associated with his concept of conatus.

Spinoza's treatment of the unity of mind and body stresses the dynamic activity of finite modes of substance, and how that activity can be enhanced or impeded by the inter-relations of those modes. That dynamism, Jaquet observes, is for Spinoza inherent both in substance and in its modes, so that, 'whether in God or in humans, there is an equality between the power of thinking and the power of acting'.[3]

Pursuing that suggestion, the expression – or realisation – of substance in thought is one and the same as its realisation in matter; or, as we might say, the one is 'at the same time' the other. Rather than a rigid correspondence between parallel series, which brings its own associations with dualism, Spinoza's two 'orders' might then be construed as different ways of conceiving the same reality – united through the inter-relations of the power to act and the products of that power.

That nuanced distinction between the power to act and its products echoes Spinoza's earlier distinction, in *Ethics I*, between Nature as *Natura Naturans* and as *Natura Naturata*. There, too, the distinction hinged on two different ways of conceiving what is one and the same 'Nature' – as productive force or as the products of that force.

Jaquet's analysis fits neatly many remarks that Spinoza makes throughout the *Ethics* on the unity of minds and bodies.[4] It also

---

[3] Ibid. 18.

[4] There is, of course, more that might be said to give content to this dif-

accords with the treatment he goes on to offer of the distinctions between human passions and the actions of the mind, associated with reason. For example, there is this passage, where he relates that distinction to his previous talk, at EIIP7 of the two orders:

> The Mind and the Body are one and the same thing, which is conceived now under the attribute of Thought, now under the attribute of Extension. The result is that the order, or connection, of things is one, whether nature is conceived under this attribute or that; hence the order of actions and passions of our Body is, by nature, at one with the order of actions and passions of the Mind. (EIIIP2Schol.)

There is much that remains unresolved about the differences among current interpretations of Spinoza's notion of expression and consequent differences in understanding his version of reason. The tensions between different ways of positioning reason in relation to the whole of Nature play out throughout the entire work – finding a resolution, of sorts, in the profound but elusive passages on the mind's eternity, which conclude *Ethics* V.

In offering a reading of Spinoza oriented towards contemporary issues, I have emphasised one side of those tensions in Spinoza's treatment of reason. My discussion has focused mainly on interpreting Spinoza's views on theoretical understanding – on reason's access to truth about the natures of things. There is a related issue of textual interpretation, which concerns more practical aspects of reason – its role in well-lived human lives, whether individual or collective. In that context, some commentators have argued – in tune with the description of Spinoza as a 'rationalist' – that he offers a modern version of the ancient ideal of the Stoic,

> ference between 'ways of talking' of the same thing. In an alternative approach to the critique of 'parallelism', Karolina Hübner has offered an illuminating interpretation of Spinoza's version of the relation between body and mind as an identity of a thing and its 'representational' being. The distinction is thus cast in terms of a thing existing in two different ways. Hübner's argument draws on an old philosophical distinction between 'formal' and 'objective' reality which, as she notes, Spinoza himself evokes in some of his talk of 'the mind of God'; see Hübner 2020.

committed to an idealised detachment from the subjectivity of imagination and emotion.

Spinoza as a Modern Stoic?

It is uncontroversial to see Spinoza as committed to the ideal of a life lived under the guidance of reason, broadly understood. He endorses detachment from short-term pleasures associated with the passions. It is also clear that for him the good life involves trying to live free of the distorting illusions of unschooled imagination. Yet the upshot of those themes is disputed in philosophical commentary on Spinoza's treatment of the relations between reason, imagination and emotion.

In his book *Think Least of Death*, Stephen Nadler has offered a nuanced reading of Spinoza, which gives due emphasis to his insistence that human minds are subjected to the necessities of Nature, while yet taking him to offer an ideal of the good life which 'resembles to a remarkable degree, in both its general contours and in its details, the life of the Stoic sage'.[5] The contrasts with my own reading are in part a matter of emphasis; yet they play out in different treatments of the upshot of Spinoza's affirmation of the power of reason.

For Nadler, Spinoza's idealised 'free person' is not an impossible ideal: 'It is neither a self-contradictory concept – a human being who is outside of Nature and not subject to the passions – nor a nomological impossibility, ruled out by the laws of nature'.[6] Nadler acknowledges that this ideal is extraordinarily difficult to attain, much less to sustain over the course of a lifetime. Yet, he argues, it remains – for Spinoza and for 'us' – 'the natural and necessary object of our most profound desire, and something that we can hope to achieve, at least in principle'.[7]

In keeping with that exalted aspiration, Nadler's interpretation of Spinoza's account of the status of reason in relation to intuitive knowledge also has a different emphasis from the one I have

---

[5] Nadler 2020: 63.
[6] Ibid. 186–7.
[7] Ibid. 187.

offered. On his reading, access to individual essences through intuitive knowledge is presented as a superior insight into the laws which determine the inter-relation of finite modes, yielding a fuller knowledge of the mind's own nature.

For Spinoza, Nadler argues, it is through thus increasing its store of 'adequate' ideas that a human mind is able to overcome the fear of death. Such a mind comes to realise that what 'remains' after death will be those adequate ideas – occurring in the mind of God, though no longer constituting the essence of itself as an individual. Hence, Spinoza's intuitive knowledge – though directed to individuals – remains centred on understanding the natures of things, and the general laws determining their inter-relations.

What becomes of imagination and emotion on such a reading of Spinoza's affirmation of reason? Nadler acknowledges both the differences that separate Spinoza from Stoic sources on the ideal of detachment, and the differences within those sources themselves. He stresses, for example, Spinoza's own insistence that it is the affective aspect of rational understanding that yields power over the passions. Yet the shadow of the austere persona of the 'Stoic sage' falls heavily on this reading of Spinoza – even if only as a rational aspiration.

On Nadler's reading, Spinoza presents a human life as finding its highest satisfaction in a mind's coming to understand itself as participating in a pre-existing rational order of Nature. That aspiration, as articulated by Nadler, does not yet amount to a model of the supremacy of humanity within Nature. Yet it does seem to find in Spinoza's philosophy the preconditions of that way of thinking – a facilitation of later developments in intellectual history, which delivered that confidence in human progress along the high road of reason.

My own reading separates Spinoza's version of the well-lived human life more sharply from that represented by the persona of the 'Stoic sage'. It also separates Spinoza's philosophy more sharply from later versions of 'rationalism'. That strand in later philosophy has, in some ways, continued the Stoic aspiration to a way of thinking that mirrors a rational order inherent in Nature. On Nadler's reading, a residue from that Stoic ideal remains possible and desirable to achieve, difficult and rare though its sustained attainment may be.

On my own reading, the model of the Stoic sage cannot be reconciled with Spinoza's insistence that human minds are essentially embedded in the totality of Nature, and that they exist only as being thus immersed within that totality. Spinoza – thus read in the Anthropocene – becomes not part of the problem of the assumed supremacy of human reason, but rather part of its solution.

Either reading of Spinoza can yield insights relevant to better contemporary understanding of ideals of reason inherited from past philosophy. However, I think that, in the context of contemporary predicaments of human presence on a changing planet, there is more to be gained by highlighting Spinoza's significant departures from the exultation in reason, epitomised in the figure of the 'Stoic sage'.

Spinoza's philosophy can then offer a model for the integration of reason, imagination and emotion – a way of thinking that facilitates a more effective response to the challenges of climate change. With that shift there remains, of course, a significant role for reason. Yet, in keeping with the reading of Spinoza's philosophy that I have offered, the key player becomes imagination.

Whatever readers themselves make of Spinoza's conclusions, thinking through the tensions between competing interpretations can of itself yield insight into the conceptual complexities in contemporary attempts to rethink human presence in Nature.

Freedom and Nature

The conceptual complexity of positioning reason in relation to Nature affects also the 'Nature' side of that dichotomy, and the way it is construed in relation to Spinoza's treatment of freedom and necessity. I have argued that, for Spinoza, true freedom comes not from being exempt from the laws governing the rest of Nature, but through reaching a deeper understanding of the truth of the interdependence of powers. Yet that Spinozist rethinking of freedom can itself be seen as reproducing the tensions within his treatment of reason. Human freedom and human reason seem to be two sides of the same problematic coin.

Here again, there are differences among recent interpretations of the upshot of Spinoza's philosophy in a contemporary context. In an essay on 'Freedom and Nature', originally published in 2016, and republished in 2020 in her collection *Learning to Live Together*, Susan James has offered a thought-provoking application of Spinoza's political philosophy to the consideration of human resilience in the face of natural disasters. She suggests that what Spinoza has to say in his political writings about liberty, tyranny and servitude can be extended to apply to humanity's place in the realm of Nature.

James observes that, in both cases, Spinoza's treatment of the inter-relations of freedom and necessity provides a basis for resistance to 'servitude'. The affect he calls fortitude can be displayed either through resistance to political tyranny, or in the context of states trying to 'protect themselves from the arbitrary power of the natural environment'.[8] She suggests that readers can take from Spinoza the insight that the key to living well in that natural environment is to learn to distinguish situations where it is appropriate to try to subject natural things to our power from those where we must adapt our way of life to the "ineluctable forces of nature".[9]

There is something appealing about this suggestion. Clearly, Spinoza did try to integrate his account – in the *Ethics* – of the well-lived human life into his treatment – in the political writings – of political power and resistance. His treatment of fortitude can be brought to bear on struggles with catastrophic natural disasters, whatever their cause.

Yet increased awareness of the impacts of human-induced climate change seems to be in dissonance with talk of the 'arbitrary power of the natural environment'. Human struggle with 'forces of nature' – in the form of catastrophic fires, floods or rising sea levels – must now take into account the past role of human agency in shaping contemporary crises. In that context, there seems something anomalous in the idea of human resistance being marshalled against a 'tyrannous' Nature.

---

[8] James 2020: Chapter 11.
[9] Ibid. 179–80.

On James's version of Spinozist resistance, 'struggling to release ourselves from the destructive powers of natural forces can make us more free'.[10] However, those first-person plurals may well carry different connotations across the inequalities between cultures that have benefited from past colonial appropriation of 'natural' resources, and those living in the scarred environments left behind by that exploitation. What is to count as 'natural' forces where past political power has left local resources depleted, and environments despoiled?

Here again, there are issues that arise from the different times and social contexts in which philosophical texts can be read. What at one time might be read as a timeless philosophical ideal may later resonate with the poignancy of lost possibilities. Catastrophic 'natural' disasters may be appropriately addressed with Spinozist fortitude. Yet, in the context of climate change, they also elicit demands for recognition of past injustices, which have exacerbated inequalities and selectively diminished human futures.

In the next chapter, I will explore some ways in which insights from Spinoza can be brought more directly to bear on rethinking the context of human presence which has come to be known as the 'Anthropocene'. In present times, increased understanding of climate science comes together with increasingly dramatic changes that are inter-related with climate change. They include mass movements of people; impacts of past colonisation on Indigenous peoples; the global effects of changed inter-relations of human and non-human 'habitat'. Past philosophical thought has played a role in how those issues are conceptualised. Bringing Spinoza into contact with current debates may help rethink the present and better imagine the future.

---

[10] Ibid. 170.

7
Rethinking the Present

The longevity of the Cartesian model of knowing confirms the strength of Spinoza's own analysis of ways in which the fixity of mental pictures can obstruct the clarity of understanding. Often, the doggedness of human imagining is a harmless and unavoidable residue from the past. Yet it can also obstruct the assimilation and dissemination of new ways of thinking. In the context of climate change, it may serve to inhibit constructive thinking and practical response.

On the Spinozist model of human presence in Nature, thought is itself immersed in the wholeness of the natural world. Human minds glimpse that wholeness of Nature from within, in confused imaginings that are then refined by reason. Yet that notion of a wholeness of Nature itself rests on changeable, contingent ways of imagining, which themselves have a history. Spinoza's articulations of wholeness date from a period before the development of sciences which can now give that idea clearer content.

Increased awareness of the basic tenets of climate science has brought a deeper sense of the wholeness of the planet and of its climate system. That wholeness now seems such an obvious truth that it can go unremarked that the very idea of the earth as an interconnected whole – and of its climate system as globally interconnected – are significant developments in intellectual history. Sarah Dry, in her study of the history of climate science, *Waters of the World*, tracks those developments through convergences of different subject areas and methods of inquiry. She argues that what may now seem self-evident has in fact been a contingent hard-won outcome of successive ways of seeing the world.[1]

A familiar 'Cartesian' spatial imagining of human presence in Nature can block insight into the contingency of ways in which thought can be construed as meeting reality. That can happen in relation to understanding developments in Western science, as well as in cross-cultural differences in thinking of human presence.

Thought and Reality: Imagining Differently

The complex conceptual issues arising around different ways of understanding the relations between thought and reality have been well articulated by Geoffrey Lloyd in a book – and related essay – on analogical thinking, and its bearing on cross-cultural knowledge systems.[2] He challenges the familiar notion of a mind-independent reality awaiting investigation. That notion, he suggests, reflects deep-seated assumptions that evade critical examination. 'The idea that there is an external reality out there to which access is possible unmediated by theories and preconceptions is a chimera.'[3] There is, he argues, no such single, given reality; we should instead think of reality itself as multidimensional.

In response to that seemingly counterintuitive proposal, it may well seem plausible to insist that such multidimensionality surely resides in ways of thinking, rather than in the objects of thought. However, that response can itself be seen as reflecting the imaginative power of the underlying model of thought and reality that is under challenge.

Lloyd's challenge to that familiar model is not inspired by Spinoza. Nor was he considering conceptual aspects of climate change. He is concerned with alternative ways of construing reality, which may not be aligned with a dominant culture. Yet his discussion does serve to reinforce some of Spinoza's claims about the situation of human minds-within-world. Considering it can help bring Spinoza's critique of the Cartesian model of human know-

---

[1] Dry 2019: 9.
[2] G. E. R. Lloyd 2015, 2017.
[3] G. E. R. Lloyd 2015: 89.

ing into closer connection with contemporary climate change discourse.

To press the claims of alternative knowledge systems is often to attract counterclaims that the objectivity of truth is here being brought under challenge from a specious 'cultural relativism'. Lloyd argues persuasively that objectivity can be maintained without being preoccupied by a misconceived ambition to arrive at a single definitive account of reality. A pluralistic approach to explanation need not endorse the idea that truth is merely subjective opinion. Explanations may draw on different metaphysical systems that divide reality up in different ways. The deeper the level of conceptual difference, the more tenuous becomes the model of a mind-independent reality awaiting human categorisation.

Lloyd's arguments suggest that explanations may differ, not only in the conclusions they reach, but at a deeper level – in the kinds of investigation they bring to the task of understanding. It is possible to be led astray by the kinds of question formulated, no less than in the answers offered. It is interesting to reflect here on Spinoza's critique of the Cartesians on the metaphysics of substance, attributes and modes, where radically different ways of dividing up reality are at play, rather than mere terminological disagreements.

The consideration of alternative knowledge systems raises also another issue that is relevant to Spinoza's critique of Descartes: the claims of deductive reason, as against those of analogical thinking, associated with imagination. Lloyd's extensive discussion of the significance of analogical thinking echoes some aspects of older philosophical debates about reason's relations with imagination, which are replayed in Spinoza's repudiation of the Cartesians.

Descartes's model of human knowing lingers in a common construal of reason as having, in principle, privileged access to the real natures of things. The processes of deductive reason are regarded as capable of laying bare definitively, as it were, the bones of reality – the underlying structures, which can subsequently be embellished by imagination in diverse ways, eliciting a range of emotional responses.

Spinoza's more integrative approach to human thinking shows the contingency of that common way of thinking of reason.

Reason's presumed definitive access to reality can be seen as itself an exercise of philosophical imagination, offering just one way of construing the presence of human thought in Nature.

Spinoza's critique of Descartes centres on the supposed dualism of mind and body. However, it also challenges a related dualism of thought and reality, which underlies assumptions about the status of reason, which have persisted into contemporary ways of thinking. To acknowledge distinctions between reason, imagination and emotion is not thereby to accept that they are ordered in a hierarchy of functions, in which reason alone has access to the one and only ultimate structure of reality.

Recognising the substantive role of imagination in knowing – along with the embedding of emotion within supposedly higher mental processes – can bring insight into the contingency of established ways of thinking of reason. In relation to climate change, one of the most significant areas for reflection, in relation to pluralism in 'cross-cultural' perspectives, is the relevance of Indigenous knowledge systems to pressing issues such as the management of land, water and fire – and, more generally, towards the very idea of 'Nature'.

Cross-Cultural Understanding and Indigenous Knowledge

Indigenous ideas of country are often construed by non-Indigenous as mere 'storytelling'. That construal can frame difference in a way that already assigns to 'Western' theorising a superior role, in relation to which Indigenous thought takes on a subordinate status. It fails to recognise that Indigenous stories are often the repository in collective memory of detailed knowledge.

What is treated by the non-Indigenous as mythology – associated perhaps with cultural ceremony or ritual – often communicates knowledge gained through generations of experience of living in specific locations. There can be also a deeper level of misconstrual, for Indigenous country – as a way of thinking of land – is not sharply separated out from other non-human parts of Nature.

Some of the complexities here have been articulated by Lesley Head in her analyses of the challenge of communicating about climate change, across difference, in an Australian context – where 'the battle to include humans in conceptualisations of nature is not yet won'. She observes that many Indigenous communities 'are still struggling against environmental management regimes that ignore or erase their presence in the landscape', while at the same time settler Australians still broadly understand themselves as 'outside' Nature.[4]

There is something deeper at stake here than two different ways of imagining relationship with neutrally construed 'land'. Indigenous country is sentient: imbued with human presence, entwined with plants, animals, ancestral beings – and the cosmos. That sense of human presence involves agency as well as knowledge. Contrary to common settler beliefs that Australia's precolonial inhabitants did not change or influence their natural 'environment', Indigenous country has long been shaped by human engagement and ingenuity.

Increasingly, in Australia, there is archaeological evidence of the impact of that long human presence and agency over more than 60,000 years. The implications of that radically increased timeline are yet to be absorbed by non-Indigenous mindsets, formed in distant centres of empire, in the relatively recent late eighteenth century.

The positioning of Indigenous and non-Indigenous belief systems in relation to one another brings some distinctive challenges in colonial-settler societies. In those contexts, responsibility for the ongoing effects of Indigenous dispossession cannot be relegated to an absent imperial power, no longer in charge of governance after a local achievement of independence. The challenges are particularly pressing when – as in Australia – urgent issues of climate change must be addressed, while political issues of Indigenous autonomy and sovereignty remain unresolved.

Indigenous ecological thinking often highlights a repudiation of human 'exceptionalism' – stressing instead the interconnections of species, and human responsibility towards non-human life forms. Some of that thinking involves concepts that seem to find resonance in the thought of Spinoza. In Aotearoa-New Zealand,

[4] Head 2016: 59.

for example, Māori ethics has invoked a concept of *mauri* – a striving to persist in being, which is the animating force of both human and non-human existence. Somewhat similar ways of thinking in Australian Indigenous cultures and languages provide a basis for seeing deep interconnections between human and non-human thriving.[5]

Those ideas have found political expression in collective 'speaking as country', where Indigenous groups are involved with non-Indigenous others in collaborative engagement on issues of land, water and resource management. The practice has also been followed in some Indigenous academic writing, where authors identify themselves not under individual names, but under the culturally specific name of the land on behalf of which they speak.[6]

Some contemporary Western movements of thought – especially in French-speaking philosophy – have made explicit comparisons between concepts within Indigenous thought and themes in Spinoza's philosophy. There are complexities here that go beyond issues of interpretation. They bear on cultural sensitivities in relation to the appropriation – whether wittingly or not – of distinctive Indigenous concepts of 'thriving'. Those Indigenous motifs often have a much longer history – and local authority – than the cultural constructs drawn from Western philosophy in terms of which they have found more recent articulation.

In a subtle critique of culturally insensitive appropriation in some of those claims of affinity with Spinoza, Simone Bignall and Daryle Rigney have questioned whether the enthusiastic embrace of Indigenous thought by non-Indigenous theorists might itself rest on an eclipsing of the cultural specificity, and originality, of Indigenous concepts. They suggest that the eager absorbing of such concepts into a non-Indigenous frame might amount to a new version of *terra nullius* – a failure to acknowledge a preexisting Indigenous presence, with its own conceptualisations of human–non-human relations.[7] In that respect, the identifying of

---

[5] Bignall and Rigney 2019: 162–4.
[6] Head 2016: 66–9.
[7] Bignall and Rigney 2019: 168–9.

'Spinozist' themes in Indigenous thought can be seen as analogous to earlier colonial-settler mentality, in which Indigenous presence is seen as a lesser stage of human development, prior to the arrival of superior instantiations of humanity.

Bignall and Rigney's carefully considered criticisms of some celebrations of Indigenous thought, inspired by Spinoza, draw on more general critiques of attempts to synthesise Indigenous and non-Indigenous knowledge.[8] The challenge here is to engage in shared response to crises of climate change without rendering the original Indigenous thought imperceptible – or relegating it to a pre-conceptual space, in relation to supposedly superior non-Indigenous knowledge systems.[9]

Ethnographer Deborah Bird Rose, who did extensive fieldwork over several decades with Australian Indigenous communities, has written eloquently of the use of the term 'shimmer' to capture a Yolngu term that conveys multifaceted, adaptive pulsation across different life forms – now increasingly under threat from species extinctions. Readers of Spinoza may well see some affinities here with his talk of inter-related strivings to persist among dynamic modes. However, Rose also offers thoughtful observations on how such intercultural 'translations' should be regarded: the challenge is to engage in fruitful encounter and transformation – a kind of reciprocal capture – while avoiding absorption.[10]

Whatever cross-cultural affinities might be found, insights drawn from Spinoza remain within a European frame. Articulating them in the contested cultural and political contexts of postcolonial societies risks reinforcing an unexamined presumption of universality. Such presumptions of cross-cultural sameness have often rendered talk of 'Enlightenment' concepts and values suspect – to those dispossessed and oppressed under colonialism, and

---

[8] They refer especially to Byrd 2011.
[9] My own thinking on these issues has drawn on the excellent discussion of colonialism in the report 'Racism and Climate (In)Justice: How Racism and Colonisation Shape the Climate Crisis and Climate Action'. See Abimbola et al. 2021.
[10] Rose 2017, 2022. She attributes the development of the idea of 'reciprocal capture' to the philosopher Isabelle Stengers, in *Cosmopolitics I*. See Stengers 2010.

disadvantaged in its aftermath. There are paradoxes of difference and sameness here that are central to understanding anomalies in postcolonial policies of 'assimilation'.

Finding affinities between Spinoza's philosophy and Indigenous knowledge systems needs to be counterbalanced by recognition that this remains an encounter across difference. It is not a matter of bringing an inchoate imagining to clearer articulation through a more sophisticated development of reason.

Indigenous understanding of country is a full and rich expression of ongoing human presence in Nature, which takes on a new significance in the context of climate change. Geoffrey Lloyd's analysis of cross-cultural perspectives can be useful here. It can be put to work in recognising that Indigenous imaginings of country are not an overlay of myths on 'land' – construed as a neutral reality awaiting a variety of interpretations.

Climate change scientists – and activists experienced in working in collaboration with Indigenous groups on country – are often more aware of the subtleties of these issues than those who theorise at a distance. There can be an implicit acceptance of Indigenous sovereignty that is enacted in practice, though it as yet eludes political acknowledgement. Initially, it may take the form, not of explicit articulation of commonalities, but of a deepened awareness of difference – expressed through respect for protocols whose authority resides in country.

Perhaps, in the context of cross-cultural perspectives amid a changing climate, what reading Spinoza can yield should not be construed as providing useful Western approximations of Indigenous concepts. It might lie in a better appreciation of the interplay of reason, imagination and emotion at the interface between 'thought' and 'reality'. That might facilitate a 'decolonising' of framing assumptions that the non-Indigenous often bring to climate change debate; and an attentive openness to very different Indigenous ways of thinking of the relations between human and non-human.

From a non-Indigenous perspective, one of the most striking features of Indigenous knowledge is its apparent lack of any sharp separation between different aspects of culture. In particular, what would readily be construed by the non-Indigenous as the realm of theoretical inquiry – of research expertise – is interwoven with storytelling, performance and ceremony.

In the context of climate change, that synthesis of what can seem from outside to be a disparate range of theory and practice – of factual knowledge and creative expression – offers a model for integrated thinking. Out of such thinking there might emerge not only new concepts, but new possibilities for effective cross-cultural communication and collaboration.

Postcolonial Imagining

In *The Nutmeg's Curse*, the novelist Amitav Ghosh traces interconnections between the depletion of local resources, Indigenous dislocation and subsequent refugee flows. The historical 'parables' narrated in that book describe the effects of colonialism in parts of the world where climate change has long been a palpable presence, rather than an abstract future possibility.[11]

In his previous book on climate change, *The Great Derangement*, Ghosh talks more generally of a crisis in current Western imagination, at the core of which is a flawed construal of human presence in the world, which impedes effective engagement with the realities of climate change. He criticises the insistence on sharp boundaries between human and non-human, which he associates with the 'Cartesian' divide between mind and matter.

More specifically, Ghosh rejects what he describes as the 'habits of thought based on Cartesian dualism that arrogate all intelligence and agency to the human while denying them to every other kind of being'.[12] That dualism, Ghosh suggests, is involved in the illusion that human beings have freed themselves from their material circumstances – to the point where they are, in effect, disconnected from bodies.

Ghosh's criticism of 'Cartesian' dualism is not offered from a Spinozist perspective. Nor is it an entirely fair critique of Descartes's model of human thought. Yet, by putting the Anthropocene into the context of Asian history, culture and literature, Ghosh is able

[11] Ghosh 2021.
[12] Ghosh 2016: 31.

to articulate ways of thinking of the non-human – and of Nature – that are often elided in Western philosophical thought. He talks of a non-Western awareness of the sublime – in which the element of terror in Nature is more salient than in more common Romantic attitudes towards the natural world. He also talks of a notion of the 'uncanny' in non-Western attitudes to the environment, associated with regarding non-human forces as able to intervene directly in human thought.

Talk of non-human forces acting on human minds can seem alien to Western thought, with its familiar celebration of human reason as transcending the wildness of Nature. Yet it need not involve anthropomorphising the non-human by treating it as capable of human-like thought. Ghosh draws on a subtle and nuanced expansion of concepts of mind and thought beyond the human, which has been offered by the anthropologist Eduardo Kohn in an ethnographical study of human presence in forests of the Ecuadorian Amazon: *How Forests Think: Toward an Anthropology Beyond the Human*, published in 2013.

Kohn's controversial approach to ethnography was also not offered from a Spinozist perspective. It was grounded in careful elaboration of a distinction formulated in C. S. Peirce's philosophy of language – between the familiar use of representative symbols, and kinds of thinking which use other ways of signifying: icons, which rely on resemblance; or indices, which reflect physical proximity. Drawing on Peirce, Kohn argues that preoccupation with symbolic representation has obscured human thought's connections with 'a broader living semiotic realm'.[13] He presents that, in turn, as a consequence of the role of dualism in creating separation between human and non-human: 'One might say that dualism, wherever it is found, is a way of seeing emergent novelty as if it were severed from that from which it emerged'.[14]

Kohn is concerned with unities across species, which continue to inform Indigenous Amazonian cultures. He also explores the residue in those cultures of colonial history – caught as 'detritus' in the forests, yielding hybrid modes of thinking, in which bound-

[13] Kohn 2013: 15–16
[14] Ibid. 57

aries are crossed between human and non-human.[15] He provocatively concludes:

> If 'we' are to survive the Anthropocene – this indeterminate epoch of ours in which the world beyond the human is being increasingly made over by the all-too-human – we will have to actively cultivate these ways of thinking with and like forests.[16]

In later comments that clarify and elaborate this controversial concept of 'sylvan thinking', Kohn has emphasised that more is at stake here than exposing an illusion of human separation from the rest of Nature, fostered by the 'Cartesian' model of thought. On his account, linguistic symbols do not merely perpetuate that separation; they serve to create it. His point is not merely that, if human thinkers had the right theoretical lens, they could see that they are not actually separated from the non-human. It is that, through the ways in which they continue to think and communicate, they are increasingly – and dangerously – actively separating themselves from the rest of Nature.

Kohn concludes that theoretical work on understanding the separation of human and non-human would be better devoted to trying to theorise their interconnections. He insists that such an expansion of capacity for thought does not involve treating other kinds of mind as human minds. What it does involve is a readiness to expand the concepts of mind and thought themselves.[17] It is a subtle and interesting point about exercises in reconceptualising human presence in the natural world.

Spinoza can be seen as offering a philosophy that allows for a theorising of connections – rather than separations – between human and non-human. On my reading, his philosophy is neither pantheist nor pan-psychic. He does not see the natural world as imbued with the presence of supernatural forces. Nor does he see its non-human parts as animated by analogues of human minds. Yet there are aspects of his philosophy which allow for conceptual

---

[15] Ibid. 183.
[16] Ibid. 227.
[17] Kohn 2014.

expansion of notions of mind and thought beyond the human species.

For Spinoza, human minds are distinctive within the totality of finite modes of thought – as ideas of human bodies. Yet those bodies are themselves not insulated from other bodily forces. His philosophy can be read as opening space for reconceptualising mind and thought in ways better attuned to the realities of cross-species interconnection on a changing planet.

It is worth noting here that Spinoza himself was willing to engage in an exercise of imagination which involved extending mind and thought beyond human embodiment. In a letter of November 1665, to his friend, the scientist Henry Oldenberg, he emphasises that he intends his analysis of the relationship between parts and wholes to apply to minds as well as bodies.

> For I maintain that there is also in nature an infinite power of thinking, which, insofar as it is infinite, contains in itself objectively the whole of Nature, and whose thoughts proceed in the same way as Nature, its object, does. Next, I maintain that the human mind is this power, not insofar as it is infinite and perceives the whole of Nature, but insofar as it is finite and perceives only the human body. For this reason I maintain that the human Mind is a part of a certain infinite intellect.[18]

That enigmatic notion of a human mind as part of an 'infinite intellect' is echoed, as we have seen, in Spinoza's talk in the *Ethics* of what he calls 'the mind of God'. What the letter to Oldenberg helps clarify is that Spinoza's treatment of a human mind as 'part of the whole of Nature' is grounded in his understanding of part and whole in relation to the physics of finite bodies. His brief comments in the letter offer a dynamic model of interacting bodily forces.

In a preceding passage, Spinoza insists that bodily wholes and parts are to be construed in terms of reciprocal agreements and adaptations:

---

[18] Curley 2016: 20.

> By the coherence of parts ... I understand nothing but that the laws or the nature of the one part adapts itself to the laws or nature of the other part so that they are opposed to each other as little as possible. Concerning whole and parts, I consider things as parts of some whole to the extent that the nature of the one adapts itself to that of the other so that they agree with one another as far as possible. But insofar as they disagree with one another, to that extent each forms in our Mind an idea distinct from the others, and therefore it is considered as a whole and not as a part.[19]

In an often quoted – and often misconstrued – analogy, he goes on to appeal to the imagining of a tiny worm lodged in the blood of a living human being. Such a worm would, he says:

> live in this blood as we do in this part of the universe, and would consider each particle of the blood as a whole, not as a part. It could not know how all the parts of the blood are regulated by the universal nature of the blood, and compelled to adapt themselves to one another, as the universal nature of the blood requires, so that they agree with one another in a definite way.[20]

What is lacked by this imagined worm, gifted with powers of perception, is not a visualisation of predetermined spatial relations within already existing larger wholes, cumulatively representing the whole of Nature. What is lacked by the human mind, evoked in the image of the worm, is insight into the interdependence of its own powers with those of other finite modes. Things appear to this mind as independent 'wholes' arrayed before it. For it does not grasp the inter-relations on which its own momentum and persistence depend.[21]

---

[19] Ibid. 18.
[20] Ibid. 19.
[21] Discussing this letter to Oldenberg, Étienne Balibar has made the interesting observation that Spinoza's points here constitute a challenge to classical philosophical understanding of the 'Whole' and the (elementary)

The lesson to be gained from this exercise in imagination is not that a human mind might be considered as like that of a worm, or vice versa. Nor is it that a mind should aspire to an impossible clear vision of the whole of Nature, laid out awaiting its contemplation. The point is that, in relation to the rest of Nature, a human mind does not itself have the status of an independent whole. Spinoza's emphasis in this letter is on a mind's felt awareness of bodily affections in reciprocal interaction with other bodies – which coincides with his definition of imagination in the *Ethics*.

All that does not of itself yield a clear content to the notion that a human mind, and its thoughts, are themselves parts of wider mind or thought, which includes non-human parts of Nature. Yet it does open up possibilities for exploring an expansion of the concepts of mind and thought – of trying to imagine what content such expansion might be given.

The exercise enacted by Spinoza's imaging of the worm in the blood raises also the issue of what constraints reason might appropriately put on such imagining. An imaginative expansion of common ways of thinking of mind and thought need not involve thinking of non-human things as 'selves'. Yet even an expansion of the concept of selfhood need not involve a dubious anthropomorphic projection from human selves. Freya Mathews, for example, has offered a reading of Spinoza's concept of conatus that allows organisms, ecosystems – and perhaps even the whole biosphere – to be construed as 'self-realising'. She argues that, thus construed, a Spinozist 'pan-psychism' might be given a new, less counterintuitive content.[22]

Spinoza and 'Post-humanism'

Reimagining the nature and limits of mind and thought has been central to a wide range of recent post-human theory. It is beyond the scope of this book to consider in detail the bearing of Spinoza

'part' as opposite extremes – evoking instead thoughts of the reciprocity and relativity of 'points of view' (Balibar 2018: 81).

[22] See the Introduction to the Routledge Classic edition of her book *The Ecological Self* in Mathews, 2021.

on the cross-currents of debate in that scholarly literature.[23] In some variants of post-humanism, the existing concept of 'human' is extended to a broader range of application. In others 'post' seems to involve the introduction of an overarching concept, under which 'human' is located as one among others. It is not always clear which of those forms of reconceptualising is involved – or whether one operates to the exclusion of the other.

In one of the most fully developed of those imaginative expansions, Donna Haraway has argued for recognition of a notion of 'companion species', in which the emotional connection between human and non-human is extended well beyond sympathetic relations between humans and pets or 'domestic' animals. Though that expansion begins from familiar cross-species connections, it offers a deep enrichment of ideas of companionship that have traditionally been more human-centred.[24]

From a different perspective, Bruno Latour has argued for a recasting of the idea of 'agency' to encompass, not only non-human, but also inanimate and constructed things – in 'assemblages' or 'networks' that change the 'natural' world.[25] Latour's conceptual constructs undercut the model of human activity exerted on the passivity of inert Nature. His version of 'ecological' recognition of interconnection involves an expansion of ideas of ecology, along with that of agency. What Arne Næss described as 'ecological attitudes' are here extended to yield a stance of 'political ecology'.

It may seem implausible to attribute agency – as Latour appears to do – to inanimate things. Yet there are some affinities here with Spinoza's treatment of the relations between human 'free' action and 'adequacy' of ideas. For Spinoza free human agency involves change that can be understood entirely through what can be encompassed in the idea of a human body. On that understanding of agency, it may well seem that, in the Anthropocene, a

---

[23] For extensive mapping of the varying forms of post-human theory, and informed commentary on the philosophical issues they raise, see Braidotti 2019, 2022.
[24] Haraway 2003.
[25] Latour 2005.

great many changes in the natural world can be attributed to wider 'assemblages' than those ideas included within that mind–body unity which is a human being. Even so, questions remain about what distinctions continue to be significant between the human and non-human constituents of such new 'assemblages' – between those that themselves think and those that do so only as part of a wider whole.

Perhaps what Spinoza has most to offer contemporary debates about the implications of reconceptualising mind, thought or agency is the insight that the celebration of distinctive human*kind* does not of itself imply or justify human 'supremacy'. Nor need 'post-human' be taken as implying 'anti-human'. Spinoza's version of 'loving-*kind*ness' might serve as a demonstration of the possibility of combining the affirmation of what is distinctively 'human' with a readiness to see its conceptual boundaries expand.

Imagining Borders

Climate change has cast a spotlight on already existing dilemmas of cross-cultural understanding and misunderstanding. It is a striking example of a kind of crisis that has local impacts, while yet requiring global solutions – epitomising the tensions between 'national interest' and concerns with the future of humanity as a whole. Amitav Ghosh's historical 'parables' in *The Nutmeg's Curse* illustrate ways in which many contemporary refugees, seeking safe pathways for recognition and resettlement, are suffering the effects of earlier colonisation – often by former imperial powers whose citizens are now insisting on strong borders.

The impacts of climate change – increasingly direct and immediate – are enmeshed with conditions that have already motivated mass movements of people. International efforts to strengthen protections for refugees and asylum seekers have been drawn into the politics of security and border protection, intensified by the Covid-19 pandemic. Many of the tensions – and much of the conceptual confusion – around those issues have centred on the powerful symbolism of borders in contemporary collective imagination.

Policies of 'strong borders' do not require real walls; metaphorical ones will suffice. Yet physical walls had been built at borders even before the introduction of stringent border controls that came with the Covid epidemic – or in anticipation of future flows of climate change refugees. Those walls have been intended not only to obstruct movement at specific locations, but to send a message – both to asylum seekers and to fearful citizens within borders – that unauthorised arrivals will not be tolerated.

Resisting the incursion of the 'unauthorised' – even those with legitimate reasons for thus arriving – has morphed into resistance to the supposed evils of people-smuggling. The term 'smuggling' in this context itself extends the reach of the symbolism of borders. Human beings, with their human strivings to persist and to thrive, have been cast as illegitimate cargo. At the same time punitive moves against the exploitation involved in the 'smuggling' has morphed into punitive treatment of the 'smuggled'.

There is an added force to the symbolism of national borders where they coincide with the separation of land from sea. Climate change can take on a stark visibility in the disappearance of beaches under coastal erosion, or the destruction of coral reefs close to shores. In nations delineated by coastal borders, that symbolism can be particularly potent in the convergence of climate change with migration issues.

John Lanchester's novel *The Wall* captures something of the imaginative power of perceptible loss of the liminal areas between land and sea, in association with the politics of border control. His fictional wall is positioned on a geographically indeterminate cliff, harshly exposed to the elements. Beaches have disappeared from this coast. Surrounded by concrete, its conscripted 'defenders' are tasked with relentless watching from lonely posts for the arrival of flotillas of alien Others. The sharpened spatial contours, and emotional bleakness, of this imagined border capture the heightened sense of anxiety directed at territorial encroachment of those construed as different in kind.[26]

In the context of climate change debate, some have argued that there is a residue of outmoded scientific theory in collective

---

[26] Lanchester 2019.

unease at unauthorised border-crossing, fanned by hostile political rhetoric. In *The Next Great Migration*, first published in 2020, Sonia Shah has traced the history of the belief that migration is a disturbance – something to be feared or prevented, rather than accepted as part of the natural order of things. She draws parallels between human and non-human mass movements of species, arguing that there are lingering effects, in contemporary attitudes to migration, of outdated assumptions around the scientific classification of kinds of living thing.

On Shah's account, current attitudes to the strengthening of borders reflects the embedding in popular consciousness of a succession of conceptual configurations that tied the understanding of species to fixed identities and locations. Most notably, she argues that rigid Linnaean taxonomies, articulated in the eighteenth century, have fostered a persistent imagining of migration as a disruptive force. Those taxonomies, she suggests, set the scene for ways of theorising population growth and control, in which human migration was cast as yielding a dangerous merging of biologically distinct groups of people. On her analysis, what began as a system of classification – which assumed sharply delineated identities – lingers in contemporary rhetoric of incursion by dangerous 'Others'.[27]

Conceptual configurations from past philosophy often underlie contemporary political rhetoric. Past ways of conceptualising difference can persist in popular imagining, strengthened by emotion. Those hidden constructs of 'essence' and 'identity' can nurture the collective fear on which rhetoric of 'strong border control' often depends. Imagery associated with mass movements of people has been exploited in the political rhetoric of border security – allowing the emotional impact of human need and distress to be redirected to the imagined 'displacement' of an established national culture.

Shah's historical narrative of the residue of outdated scientific theory in popular imagining of borders does not draw on Spinoza. However, Spinoza's critique of the Cartesian model of human thought may fruitfully be brought into connection with issues

[27] Shah 2021.

raised by her analysis. The rigid categories of Linnaean classifications of species involve a spatialised – strongly visual – way of construing difference in kind. Fixity is already implicit in that configuration of thought; it is very much in keeping with the Cartesian sharp differentiation of 'clear and distinct ideas'.

It may seem far-fetched to suggest that Spinoza's dynamic version of individual essence as conatus might have potential for the exposure and critique of assumptions implicit in contemporary collective imagining of borders. Yet it does open up possibilities for alternative ways of thinking of relevant differences in kind.

Associating 'essence' with Spinozist conatus suggests greater flexibility and fluidity in processes of classification. It also carries different emotional resonances. To think of difference as dynamic, fluid – oriented to the forming of new connections – may be more congenial to an expansive approach to encounters across difference. It might encourage acceptance of the efforts of fellow humans to thrive through relocation. Treating movement into a different territory as an expression of 'striving to persist' has different emotional import from its construal as intrusion into a space somehow predetermined to be the 'natural' domain of those already there.

It is individual human beings, acting from desire for continued existence and thriving, that are affected by the exploitation of poorly understood – and often scientifically outdated – configurations of thought. Those hidden constructs can influence the formation of current border policies, and the collective fear on which their implementation often depends.

Needless to say, not all such 'unauthorised' encroachment on territory can be made acceptable through a Spinozist reimagining of unity and difference. My point here is not that philosophical insights drawn from Spinoza can be directly enlisted into the formation or implementation of migration or refugee policy. The point is that an understanding of his philosophy may help expose the contingency of habitual ways of imagining. It might open possibilities for rethinking people-movements in the Anthropocene – beyond a default readiness to treat all unauthorised border-crossing as a threat.

Political rhetoric has the power to elicit or intensify anxiety about a disintegration of fragile social structures. The anthropologist Jonathan Neale has called attention to the role here of imagery associated, especially, with the political theory of Thomas Hobbes – evoking strong state power as needed in order to keep social collapse at bay. In the imagining of catastrophic collapse, fellow human beings – in need of assistance – can be recast as enemies. Punitive state power is then construed as the bulwark ensuring security.[28] A Spinozist critique of such amalgams of imagery and political rhetoric may help to explain how international efforts directed to sharing responsibility for assisting refugees have so often been transformed into collaborations between nation-states in measures to block mass movements of people.

In offering this possible application of Spinoza's philosophical thought to contemporary debates, I acknowledge that my discussion glides over some complex issues of textual interpretation. It might be observed that, since Linnaean classifications concern species rather than individuals, they should be construed in terms of Spinoza's version of 'formal' rather than 'individual' essences; whereas it is his treatment of individual essence that is strongly linked to the concept of conatus.

An attempt to apply a philosophical text to a contemporary debate can go too far, if it relies on playing fast and loose with textual details. There is room for argument here. Yet arguments about textual interpretation can themselves be illuminating for better understanding of what is at stake in conceptual aspects of current debate. Generic and individual essences are not themselves distinct entities; they are different ways of considering the natures of individual things. Connections can plausibly be drawn between identifying supposed 'essential properties' of a general group and attitudes towards its individual members.

There are distinctive features of Spinoza's treatment of 'essence' that can be brought to bear more broadly on contemporary issues of kinds and identity. His linking of essence with conatus carries implications of concreteness rather than abstraction; and of fluidity rather than fixity. Étienne Balibar has argued that, under

---

[28] Neale 2019.

Spinoza's analysis, the metaphysical concept of essence undergoes a profound change: rather than referring only to a class or genus, it reaches towards the singularity of individuals.[29]

In the context of Spinoza's treatment of loving-kindness, reciprocal recognition of shared kind yields expansion of sympathetic connection between individuals. That might provide a template for an expansion of fellow-feeling to include those beyond the borders of a nation-state – grounded in the recognition of shared affinities, under crises that do not themselves respect political borders.

A Spinozist 'wholeness of Nature' is differently imagined from spatial models of inclusion or separation. It is construed in terms of dynamic enmeshing of strivings to persist – of powers of acting and being acted upon. The recognition of shared humanity at stake here is not the registering of an abstract identity. It is an affective response to the understanding of sameness across difference – sustained by insight into a wholeness of humankind that resonates with the wholeness of the planet itself.

---

[29] Balibar 2018: 37–8.

8
Imagining the Future

Spinoza's treatment of mind and thought is gaining increased attention, not only from philosophers, but also from contemporary scientists. Aspects of his critique of the 'Cartesian' model are echoed in attempts to communicate radical shifts in scientific thinking.

The physicist Carlo Rovelli has commented on the impossibility of drawing a complete map of everything that happens in the world, suggesting that it is instead like a collection of inter-related points of view. Thus, he says, in *The Order of Time*, to speak of the world 'seen from outside' makes no sense, because there is no 'outside' to the world.[1] Rovelli is not, there, articulating an insight dawn from Spinoza. Yet there are some parallels between his talk of 'inter-related points of view' and Spinoza's repudiation of the Cartesian model of objectivity. In his earlier book, *Seven Brief Lessons on Physics*, Rovelli explicitly invokes Spinoza in support of his own integrative view of human minds and their freedom.

> There is not an 'I' and 'the neurons in my brain'. They are the same thing. An individual is a process: complex, tightly integrated . . . I am, as Spinoza maintained, my body and what happens in my brain and heart, with their immense and, for me, inextricable complexity.[2]

---

[1] Rovelli 2018: 108–9.
[2] Rovelli 2015: 71–3.

Contemporary researchers in the biological sciences have also remarked on some affinities of their work with Spinoza's alternative model of human knowing, as well as with his more familiar rejection of Descartes's dualism of mind and body.[3] In an explicit acknowledgement of the significance of Spinoza's departure from Cartesian assumptions, Denis Noble has drawn on that Spinozist model in articulating the upshot of recent concepts of 'biological relativity'.[4]

Of particular interest, in relation to current climate change discussion, is new engagement from contemporary philosophers and scientists with Spinoza's treatment of what he calls the affects – the desires, impulses and emotions that are a central feature of human lives. However, it is not just theoretical inquiry into those affective states that can draw insights from reading Spinoza. There are aspects of his writing – not just of its theoretical content – which give contemporary relevance to his integrative approach to reason, imagination and emotion.

A crucial aspect of response to climate change is the effective communication of complex issues to a general audience. That demands not just clarity and accessibility, but also imaginative engagement with the emotions associated with climate change. Here, it is significant that Spinoza's works, daunting though they can appear, have often had a direct appeal – not only to philosophers and scientists, but also to readers more oriented to literature and the creative arts.

Spinoza's Writing

Gilles Deleuze, in an engaging discussion of the phenomenon of Spinoza's appeal to a non-scholarly readership, in his *Spinoza: Practical Philosophy*, talks of a common experience in reading the *Ethics*. It can exert a strong emotional appeal, even in the lack of full comprehension of its intellectual content. He articulates the

---

[3] Chantal Jaquet has discussed the significance, in the context of current research on mind–brain relations, of Antonio Damasio's *Looking for Spinoza: Joy, Sorrow and the Feeling Brain* (2003) in Jaquet 2018: 4–7.
[4] Noble 2017: 164–8, 174.

point vividly in the concluding sections of the book: 'Writers, poets, musicians, film-makers – painters too, even chance readers – may find that they are Spinozists; indeed, such a thing is more likely for them than for professional philosophers'.[5]

Deleuze goes on to say that, despite Spinoza's highly developed, systematic and scholarly conceptual apparatus,

> [H]e is the quintessential object of an immediate, unprepared encounter, such that a nonphilosopher, or even someone without any formal education, can receive a sudden illumination from him, a 'flash'. Then it is as if one discovers that one is a Spinozist; one arrives in the middle of Spinoza, one is sucked up, drawn into the system or the composition.[6]

A cynical response to that description might be that Spinoza appeals more to emotion than to clear-headed reason. Yet Spinoza has himself forestalled such easy dismissal, by his rigorously reasoned defence of his integrative treatment of the relations between reason, imagination and emotion. The emotional response may be a 'sudden illumination'. Yet it can also be seen as induced by a carefully crafted set of rigorous thought processes.

Deleuze's remarks draw, appropriately, on a novelist's articulation of the impact of reading Spinoza. He cites, as an epigraph for his book, an insight captured in a quote from a character in Bernard Malamud's novel *The Fixer*. It is possible, that character says, to be captivated, as though one reads with a whirlwind at one's back – as though one is taking a witch's ride. It is an interesting remark, which resonates with many readers of Spinoza; and there are similar responses throughout the many scattered references to Spinoza in literary works.

Deleuze elaborates his description of the emotional impact of Spinoza's writing by talking of its amenability to what he calls a 'double reading'. On the one hand, he says, the text of the *Ethics* can be read 'systematically' – in pursuit of the general idea and the unity of the parts. On the other hand, and at the same

---

[5] Deleuze 1988: 129.
[6] Ibid. 129.

time, there can be an 'affective reading, without an idea of the whole, where one is carried along or set down, put in motion or at rest, shaken or calmed according to the velocity of this or that part'.[7]

Overblown though those descriptions may sound, it is worth examining more closely this issue of the immediacy of Spinoza's appeal to modern readers, in the context of emotions generated – and sometimes transformed – under the accelerated impacts of climate change. Any philosopher can, of course, be read in a variety of ways; and there is always room for argument about the best reading. However, Deleuze's suggestion is that reading Spinoza not only admits but demands an affective reading – that readers miss the core of his writing, if they are not affected by it.

Deleuze's point is worth trying to unravel. At first sight, it may seem outlandish to suggest that a piece of philosophical writing might require an 'affective' reading. In relation to the *Ethics*, it may seem especially counterintuitive. It has, after all, often been presented as a paradigm of 'rationalist' writing – a tightly unified structure of deductive argumentation, set out in geometrical form. I want to suggest that Deleuze is nonetheless right to point to the importance of emotional engagement for grasping the full import of Spinoza's writing.

Deleuze's comments were directed to the bearing of Spinoza's thought on theory and practice in literature and the arts, rather than to any specific political or social context in which his works might be read. Yet they take on a new significance in present times, when the clear communication of scientific findings can seem inadequate to elicit collective response to the urgencies of a changing climate.

The impacts of climate change can be experienced emotionally with a directness that eludes the immediate capacity for intellectual response. At the same time, emotions themselves can undergo transformation with the collapse of accustomed ways of imagining a human future. When the future seems unimaginable, it can be difficult to think clearly about either adaptation or mitigation in the present.

[7] Ibid. 129.

I discussed earlier the influence of Spinoza – not always accurately interpreted – on the literary culture of Romanticism, which lingers in contemporary attitudes towards human presence in Nature. Yet one aspect of the affective immediacy, of which Deleuze speaks, is the powerful influence Spinoza has had even on literature that repudiates Romantic sensibility.

Jacques Derrida has discussed ways in which Spinoza's philosophy was a strong preoccupation and motivating force in the literary practice of Gustave Flaubert – despite the fact that Flaubert's *Madame Bovary* is a classic exposé of the ambiguities and ambivalences of the mentality associated with the Romantic sublime. In his essay 'An Idea of Flaubert', Derrida has assembled supporting evidence for the impact of Spinoza on Flaubert – scattered throughout his literary works and his correspondence. He argues that, despite Flaubert's frequent railing at the stupidity of philosophy – in its attempts to come up with definitive conclusions about the natures of things – there is, throughout his works, a recurring concern with fundamental philosophical issues, especially as articulated by Spinoza.[8]

Flaubert was fascinated, especially, by Spinoza's views on the presence of mind and thought within the world. Writing to George Sand, in a letter of 1870, about his reactions on first reading the *Theological-Political Treatise*, he says: 'It's dizzying! I'm in transports of admiration! *Nom de Dieu!* What a man! What a brain!'[9] In another letter of 1872, he favourably compares the experience of reading Spinoza with his reactions to reading Kant and Hegel, which he finds stupefying. 'When I leave their company', he says, 'I fall hungrily on my old, thrice-great Spinoza. What a genius! What a work, the *Ethics!*'[10]

Flaubert was capable of mocking his own enthusiasm. He put his excitement about Spinoza into the mouths of his loveable, eccentric autodidacts – the clerks Bouvard and Pécuchet. Discovering the *Ethics* – in the midst of their disaster-ridden pursuit of knowledge – they are fascinated, but also frightened. Reading Spinoza, they felt:

---

[8] Derrida 2007.
[9] Flaubert to Sand, 29 April 1870, in Steegmuller and Bray 1993: 196–7.
[10] Flaubert to Sand, 31 March 1872, ibid. 269.

as if they were in a balloon, at night, in the glacial cold, carried along in an endless rush toward a bottomless abyss – with nothing around them but the ungraspable, the immobile, the eternal. It was too much. They gave up.[11]

Derrida rightly suggests that it is recognition of a shared artistic vision that makes Flaubert embrace Spinoza. Flaubert was not interested in following the theoretical detail of the *Ethics*. At that level, like Bouvard and Pécuchet, he was prepared to give up. Flaubert is not a 'Spinozist' – if that means being intellectually convinced by the argumentation through which Spinoza seeks to establish his metaphysics. Yet he is enthralled by the vision of embodied minds, which come to understanding within the totality of the world; and he is struck by the limitations that situation imposes on human knowing. For Flaubert, Spinoza – rather than purporting to definitively describe the world, as if from an external viewpoint – celebrates the inherent partiality of human thought. He attempts to express that Spinozist vision of mind and world in his own artistic practice.

There is an important insight here into a tension that arises also for those who read Spinoza in a contemporary context. On the one hand, his writing evokes a realm of 'the ungraspable, the immobile, the eternal' – as the narrator of *Bouvard and Pécuchet* puts it. On the other hand, it evokes a poignant sense of an individual mind, struggling – from within the confused totality of things – to articulate an ever-elusive truth. For Flaubert, Spinoza speaks to that sense of the artist as giving form to an inchoate apprehension of something-they-know-not-what.

That sense of trying to articulate something from within the whole is central to the content of the *Ethics*, though it may pull against its form. The convergence of intellect, imagination and emotion, striving for expression, is for Spinoza what it is to be a human mind. That Spinozist model of mind-in-world speaks powerfully to a contemporary sense of the inadequacy of intellect alone to fully articulate the deep sense of unease that comes from awareness of the finitude of human thought within a changing planet.

[11] Flaubert 2005: 193.

Spinoza's treatment of reason helps make sense of the limitations of theoretical discourse in the challenge of communicating the urgent truths of climate change to minds apparently resistant to scientific consensus. It helps understand how the most effective communication on climate change may involve more than the clear communication of established facts.

For Spinoza, reason is effective against mental passivity only because it can be itself affective. In his philosophy, as we have seen, reason's traditional hierarchical relationship to imagination and emotion is transformed. Supposedly lesser aspects of mind are incorporated, rather than left behind.

Climate scientists and activists are increasingly collaborating with creative writers and artists to achieve more effective communication of their understanding of a changing reality. Spinoza's treatment of the inter-relations and interactions of reason, imagination and emotion can deepen insight into why that collaboration is important. It is not just a matter of popularising the content of theoretical research. It is an approach that speaks to human minds, whose own nature involves those fluctuations of reason, imagination and emotion.

Spinoza's integrative model of the mind points also to ways in which human emotions are themselves changing in a new context. It opens possibilities of imaginative thinking, attuned to those transformations. That fits well with current reflections on collaborative interaction in response to climate change – across the borders of academic disciplines, and across some of the habitual boundaries that separate theorising and practice in science, the arts and literature.

Science Fiction and Climate Change

The sense of futurity is at the core of climate change emotion. It is not surprising, then, that contemporary literature that addresses climate change often takes the form of fictional scenarios of a projected future. John Lanchester's *The Wall*, which I mentioned earlier, positions its narrator at an indefinite point in an imagined future, which has recognisable points of connection with a familiar present.

The Wall is set beyond the occurrence of an unspecified 'Change', which has dramatically shifted the parameters of citizens' lives. Day-to-day existence is shaped by a pervasive preoccupation with the feared arrival of unspecified Others. The bleak Wall, on which the novel's characters carry out their compulsory service of security surveillance, is a harsh spatial border; but it also symbolises the chasm that separates present from past. It is the continuities of human feelings across that temporal rupture that give the novel its emotional power.

Imaginative play with futuristic scenarios has of course been central to a whole genre of modern literature – science fiction. In his discussion, in *The Great Derangement*, of the current crisis in Western forms of narrative imagination, Amitav Ghosh noted that, although contemporary writers very often write about climate change as an issue of concern, they rarely address it in their own works of creative fiction. When novelists do choose to write about climate change, he observed, they almost always do so outside of fiction. Climate change, on Ghosh's account, has been relegated to the genre of science fiction – that is, to preoccupation with extraterrestrial or interplanetary travels.[12]

It was a controversial observation, which appeared to relegate contemporary science fiction to non-serious concoction of futuristic fantasies. For lovers of the genre, science fiction has always been more than an indulgence in bizarre fantasy; and, for lovers of the genre of fantasy, that too can be much more than mere escape from reality.

One of the most interesting developments in contemporary creative writing, in the context of climate change, has come with science fiction's capacities to bring imagined futures into engagement with present realities. The genre's long fascination with time, especially, has now taken on an orientation towards themes related to climate change.

In a wide range of novels and short stories, the Chinese science fiction writer Liu Cixin has brought the intricacies of contemporary physics and technology together with fiction, in an interplanetary context. In his trilogy *The Three-Body Problem*, published

---

[12] Ghosh 2016: Part I.

from 2006 to 2010, political conspiracies and conflicts unfold, over cosmic distances and across light years, impinging on familiar earthly settings on a changing planet. Liu's work brings familiar emotional nuances in earthly human social relations together with accessible articulation of complex issues in contemporary science. That is a common conjunction in recent science fiction, much of which engages explicitly with both the science of climate change and its emotional impacts.

The Australian novelist James Bradley has observed that the way the future is imagined has always been about the ways the present is understood.[13] Imaginative depicting of emotional continuities between past and future can act as an expression of hope. The scenarios offered in science fiction are not confined to catastrophic dystopias. They may depict ways in which humanity persists – futures of adaptation and resilience, as well as of catastrophic social collapse.

Bradley's own novel, *Clade*, is set in a future the unfolding of which is recognisable, though clearly somewhat beyond the reader's present.[14] The succession of events throughout the lives of characters ensure that adaptation is visible, no less than the shock of radical change. Emotions unfold from a recognisable present into that uncertain future. New patterns of relationship develop, captured as variants on the old, through an unstated metaphor, drawn from the biological term which gives the novel its title, 'clade' – the evolutionary descendants of a common ancestor.

One of the most prolific and successful writers of contemporary science fiction, the American novelist Kim Stanley Robinson, has also commented on that interconnection of future and present. He goes further, suggesting that science fiction, engaging as it does with new 'structures of feeling', can be seen as the literary realism of present times; its scenarios are no longer relegated to an abstract, distant future. In relation to a changing planet, 'we' can increasingly be seen as ourselves living in the unfolding future of a past in which mitigating action was possible, but was not taken.[15]

[13] Bradley 2020b.
[14] Bradley 2015.
[15] Robinson 2020a.

In Robinson's novel, *The Ministry for the Future*, published in 2020, imagining the future becomes, not just a way of understanding a fearful present, but also an exercise in sustaining precarious hope. Here, science fiction becomes a richly multi-genre exercise, with chapters moving between an unpredictable array of different voices. Depictions of grief, rage, acceptance, hope and love are intertwined with theoretical reflection. Some voices narrate fictional eye-witness accounts of climate catastrophe located in a near future; others speak in the more detached tones associated with informed scientific understanding. On occasion, a teasing voice erupts from the cosmos, identifying itself as an observing photon.

The Ministry for the Future is as much an informative summation of current climate change politics as it is an engaging work of fiction. It enacts the author's notion of a new 'structure of feeling' – an idea derived from Raymond Williams – as a concept of difference in the configuration of emotions throughout cultural change. In one chapter, in the literary genre of discursive essay, a voice talks of climate change as bringing a 'cultural shaping' of the present.[16] In another, a meditative voice tentatively relates that new 'structure of feeling' to a new way of thinking, which tries to give content to the idea of humanity being part of a whole: 'All of us in balance, we the people, meaning we the living beings, in a single eco-system which is the planet ... Maybe this makes us all living together in this biosphere some kind of supra-organism, who can say'.[17]

This new 'structure of feeling', as the notion is articulated in the novel, is not an abstract theoretical concept. It seems to be something akin to Spinoza's affective knowing – a kind of joy. The imagined voice continues: 'whether life means anything or not, joy is real. Life lives, life is living'.[18]

The plot of *The Ministry for the Future* unfolds in a future perilously close to the book's present. Yet its concerns are continuous with Robinson's earlier exercises in the genre, which are more

---

[16] Robinson 2020b: 124.
[17] Ibid. 502.
[18] Ibid. 502.

conventionally futuristic. In his previous novel, *New York 2140*, published in 2017, climate-related sea rises have put large parts of New York City under water. The book's interlocking plots centre on characters living precariously, above water, in a residential housing cooperative.

Those plots unfold against a background of unscrupulous landlords, real estate speculation and ever-expanding tiers of transnational corporations, which exploit and subvert structures of local government. Yet the daily lives of the characters, drawn from a wide variety of the city residents, continue – in recognisable patterns of desire, hope and frustration – amid the rising skyscrapers soaring over their 'new Venice'. What is offered here is not a frightening dystopian vision of the future. It is a realistic, scientifically informed, yet hopeful vision of positive possibilities amid tragic potentialities.

Many of the themes explored in *New York 2140* and *The Ministry For The Future* are familiar from Robinson's prescient *Mars Trilogy*, published from 1992 to 1996, the plots of which unfold over a vaster time scale, yet remain sharply attuned to an earthly present. A multiethnic group of pioneering Mars colonisers, whose lives are extended through gerontological treatments, coexist there with their youthful Martian descendants – along with more recent arrivals from a depleted and crisis-ridden Earth.

Over a long span of Earth-centuries, these Martian communities develop passionately held and conflicted visions of human presence on Mars. They are, though, united, in resistance to the power of earthly transnational corporations that are intent on exploiting the mineral resources of the planet. The tensions on Mars unfold in a succession of revolutions and ensuing civil divisions – intermittently influenced by current crises on Earth.

Much of the political division depicted in the *Mars Trilogy* centres on differing approaches to the imagining of human presence on a planet which has existed for aeons without that presence. Echoing some of the concerns of twentieth-century Environmental Philosophy, these novels ask such questions as: should Mars be construed as itself having 'rights'? Does its stark inherent beauty depend for its value on the presence of human consciousness to apprehend it? Should Mars, for the sake of human thriving, be terraformed in the likeness of Earth? Or should these colonisers of Mars instead transform themselves – adapting their needs and desires to the planet's own distinctive nature?

Clearly, these novels are serious exercises in imaginative thinking about the complexities of human presence on an Earth challenged by climate change; they are not merely escapist fantasies about travel to another planet. Contemporary science fiction increasingly speaks to the need for new ways of thinking about – and emotionally responding to – present issues of climate change on the one planet as yet amenable to human presence. Where it shifts attention to an imagined future, it does so not simply to entertain, but to better understand the present.

Spinoza's Ingenium and the Human Future

Fiction is more directly engaged than nonfiction with the understanding and communication of imagination and emotion. Yet much of the engagement of contemporary fiction with climate change issues has intellectual depth that goes beyond reverberation of emotion. There are in it recurring motifs that resonate with some of the themes from Spinoza's philosophy which I have tried to relate to present times: the struggle of human minds for ever better understanding from within the totality of being; the distortions of flawed imagining that impede those efforts; the structural interconnections of reason, imagination and emotion; the centrality of joy to the well-lived human life; the power of affect in human collectivities.

The 'sudden illumination' that Deleuze described as a common response to reading Spinoza is not an incidental 'flash' of emotion. It reflects a theme that runs through the intellectual content of Spinoza's writing: his emphasis on the affective aspects of human knowing. It is what might be expected of a mind which, of its nature, is ever striving for better understanding from within the totality of being. It reflects Spinoza's own efforts to articulate the insight that human thought is inherently part of the reality it seeks to understand. There is something peculiarly appropriate about that insight to the times in which Spinoza is now read.

In his political writings, Spinoza talks of a concept he calls 'ingenium', the broad meaning of which is a characteristic arrangement of affects. Spinoza uses the concept in talking of a distinctive interplay of emotions, specific to an individual. He also extends it as a way of focusing on the prominence of particular passions within different human collectivities. On his analysis, that distinctive affective character of a people finds expression in characteristic laws and structures of governance: over time, some affects take on a greater salience, while others recede from attention.

Chantal Jaquet has helpfully summed up Spinoza's ingenium as 'the lasting characteristics related to thinking habits, lifestyle and history, which make an individual or people recognisable by distinguishing them from others'.[19] There is a strong temporal element in that rendering of the concept – a people's historical experience will play a significant role in determining its ingenium.

The notion of 'structures of feeling', which Kim Stanley Robinson borrowed from Raymond Williams, is more explicitly tied to processes of change within a particular culture – rather than to contrasts between cultures. Yet there are some similarities between the two notions. Perhaps it now makes sense to talk of a distinctive ingenium of the present – a structure of thought, imagination and feeling, which finds expression, across cultural differences, in shared recognition of the significance of climate change for human future.

Spinoza and Descartes are both rightly associated with the mentality now retrospectively appropriated as 'Enlightenment thought' – with the celebration of free pursuit of objective intellectual inquiry through the cultivation of reason. I have argued that there are, nonetheless, elements in Spinoza's thought that pull against some of the key features that have come to be associated with that mentality.

Perhaps his philosophy now speaks to a different 'structure of feeling' from that epitomised in Descartes's model of human knowing, which was centred on a sharp separation of human minds from the rest of Nature.

---

[19] Jaquet 2018: 31–2.

The hesitant formulation, by the narrator of *Ministry for the Future*, of such concepts as the unity of the biosphere – construed as a kind of 'supra-organism' – may be, as yet, no less baffling to contemporary readers than Spinoza's talk of a mind coming to understand itself as part of the 'mind of God'. Yet the search for appropriate analogies or metaphors responds to a deep sense of unease with more familiar ways of construing human presence in the world. That unease is as much about articulating 'structures of feeling' appropriate for present times, as it is about communicating the facts of climate change.

I have tried to present Spinoza as a fruitful source of insight in the context of current efforts to better understand the place of human thought within the 'whole of Nature' – even if the full force of his version of that wholeness remains elusive to contemporary readers. The paradox that Spinoza formulated remains appropriate: the deep truths of human existence may be accessible to all; yet their adequate understanding and articulation remains difficult to achieve. One might now add that such understanding has never been more necessary – not only for the sake of well-lived individual lives, but for the future of the human species as a whole.

Conclusion: 'Descartes' and 'Spinoza'

This book began from one seventeenth-century philosopher's attempt to refute another's theoretical treatment of the nature of human error. That dispute was framed by a deeper disagreement about the nature of the relations between human minds and bodies. Neither Spinoza nor his Cartesian opponents could have foreseen that such a disagreement might play out, centuries later, in contested construals of the presence of humanity on a perilously changing planet.

Descartes's treatment of mind–body relations is now frequently mentioned in critiques of what is seen as a 'Western' way of conceptualising human relations with the rest of Nature. His model – emphasising separation – is invoked as an obstacle to adequate understanding of the issues at stake in anthropogenic global warming. The figure of Descartes hovers as a ghostly target of challenges to the depiction of human beings as polarised from the non-human, and of Nature itself as an 'it' polarised from 'us' – as something wild to be tamed or conquered; or as an inert resource for active human exploitation.

That figure of 'Descartes' is in some ways itself a construct of imagination. While it does fit with some things actually written by the real Descartes, it also bypasses many nuances in the historical texts. Talk of Cartesian 'separatism' overlooks the carefully crafted rhetorical structure of Descartes's best known work, his *Meditations*. Famously, he enacted – in the second Meditation – a radical separation of mind and body, grounded in a rigorous process of subjecting all things to doubt. Yet that separation was supposed to be offset in the sixth, concluding Meditation, by his description of a more porous intermixing.

It is not surprising that, once mind and body had been so radically separated, Descartes's attempt to unify them across difference was seen as incoherent. His attempt to reunite mind and body was rightly challenged by some of his contemporaries – not only by Spinoza, but also in the lesser known, gentle yet powerful, critique offered in letters from Descartes's friend Elisabeth, Princess of Bohemia.

It was the rigid separation of minds and bodies – and the associated sharpness of boundaries between human and non-human – that, rightly or wrongly, became Descartes's legacy. He is commonly associated also, in present times, with mechanistic causal models of body – epitomised in his notorious view of non-human animals as mindless automata.

While in some respects accurate, that representation of Descartes is incomplete. It does not capture the subtlety of his treatment of the bodily aspects of human emotions in his remarkable final work, *The Passions of the Soul*, which he dedicated to Princess Elisabeth. Although Spinoza was scathing in his repudiation of the underlying model of causal interaction between material body and immaterial soul, he was clearly impressed and influenced by the descriptions of particular emotions which Descartes offered there.

The fleshly Descartes of the seventeenth century may well not have deserved his spectral survival into the twenty-first, as a symbol of human separation from Nature. Yet current critique of the 'Cartesian' model of human presence in the natural world cannot be dismissed as entirely misplaced. That model articulated a distinctive status of a human mind as a freestanding immaterial, individual substance – exerting power over the rest of Nature. It helped shape the commercial aspirations and practices of later European empires, facilitating appropriation of the natural resources of distant colonies. It helped provide justification of the exploitative trade arrangements which accompanied eighteenth-century journeys of exploration, and the dispossession of Indigenous peoples.

More generally, that Cartesian model accrued associations with ideas of Nature itself as appropriate object of human conquest and exploitation. Despite Descartes's efforts to reunite human minds with the rest of Nature, the status he had given them – as individual substances – set them apart. Cartesian minds are seen as autonomous in their separation from Nature, rather than as struggling to achieve freedom within it. The very completeness of those 'intellectual substances' was a barrier to imagining the wholeness of Nature.

Perhaps it should be no surprise that the lingering of that Cartesian model has come to fit so well with the determination to find climate change 'solutions' exclusively in yet further advances of human control of Nature – rather than through serious rethinking of old conceptual structures of separation. The negative connotations of the figure of 'Descartes' have hardened under the growing impact of contemporary critique of Western views of Nature. In that context, the neglected figure of 'Spinoza' has taken on a more positive allure.

I have offered throughout this book a reading of Spinoza's philosophy that points to a path not taken in the history of Western philosophy. It is a useful metaphor. However, it is not meant to suggest that a Spinozist path – if only it had been taken – might have yielded an entirely different outcome to the subsequent history of Western civilisation.

Although Spinoza's philosophy drew on a rich variety of intellectual sources, he too was a man of his time and place. His family belonged to an Amsterdam community, actively involved as merchants in trade with the colonies of Spain and Portugal. Although he lived a frugal scholarly life – much of it in enforced exile from Amsterdam – that life unfolded within the context of the 'Golden Age' of Dutch journeys of exploration and economic expansion. There is no reason to think he would have had any special sensitivity to the effects of those expeditions on distant peoples.

Nor, as we have seen, did Spinoza's own thinking lead him to personally question the right of human beings to exploit non-human parts of Nature. It is in reading him now, through the accretions of what came later, that his emphasis on interconnection – as against separation – yields insight into possible ways of rethinking human relations with Nature.

There are, nonetheless, aspects of Spinoza's writing – in its style and structure, as well as in its content – that do bear in important ways on current climate change discourse. His metaphysics of substance, attributes and modes makes unusual moves with concepts that are nonetheless familiar within the philosophical tradition now identified as 'Western'. Some of those sources were common to other Western philosophers, including Descartes. Yet the wide diversity of Spinoza's sources, and the use he made of them, offers to contemporary readers a rich exposure to unfamiliar and challenging ways of thinking.

I have highlighted the Stoic influence on Spinoza's treatment of emotion, and the significance of his departures from that influence. There is a complementary thread of Epicureanism in his thought.[1] There is also a strong active presence of sources less familiar to many contemporary readers – Jewish thinkers, such as Maimonides and Gersonides; and Islamic thinkers, such as Avicenna and Averroes.

That range of sources – together with the originality of Spinoza's own thought processes – ensures that there are frequent encounters with strangeness in the experience of reading Spinoza now. The conjunction of the familiar and the surprising – of continuity and disruption – is a challenge to habitual thought patterns that are exploited in contemporary political rhetoric. The very familiarity of the separatist models of mind and thought, and of human and non-human, can make what is in fact contingent seem unchangeable. That in itself can make reading Spinoza now a stimulus to rethinking human relations with Nature.

There is also something else. Daunting and uncongenial though the format of the *Ethics* may at first appear, its content engages deeply with the everyday experience of human beings, unfolding in interaction with the natural world of which they are inextricably part.

Pierre-François Moreau has written movingly of this aspect of Spinoza's writing, in his masterly study *Experience and Eternity in Spinoza*. In an interview with Robert Boncardo, the translator of

---

[1] For an interesting and informative scholarly treatment of the Epicurean strands in Spinoza's thought, see Vardoulakis 2020.

the English version of the book, Moreau observes that Spinoza's writing is 'teeming with life' – as we experience it in ourselves, as we see it in others, or as we learn about it in literary traditions, which act 'as a kind of condensation of collective experience'. All that, he says, is 'massively present' in Spinoza – not in the form of some kind of concession or afterthought, but at the very heart of his thought. 'When Spinoza is reasoning about things that are apparently abstract or rational, all of this is there in the form of examples, of material, of living flesh, underneath his thought's structures.'[2]

All this makes Spinoza's writing less dry and abstract than its form might at first suggest. It is an intellectual exercise congenial to – and enhanced by – imagination and emotion. The conjunction of the strange and the familiar in his writing – together with that sense of immediate connection with 'teeming life' – can make the experience of reading him now different from what might be expected.

A retreat to reading Spinoza in the Anthropocene might seem a quaint response to the fearful sense of human civilisation in crisis. Yet it can deepen insight into that all-too-human fear. It can bring transition to greater understanding. On Spinoza's own analysis, that can yield hope – even in the face of catastrophic change.

---

[2] Boncardo 2021: 570.

Bibliography

Abimbola, Olumide, Joshua Kwesi Aikins, Tselane Makhesi-Wilkinson and Erin Roberts (2021) 'Report: Racism and Climate (In)Justice: How Racism and Colonisation Shape the Climate Crisis and Climate Action'. Washington, DC: Heinrich Böll-Stiftung. https://us.boell.org/en/2021/03/19/racism-and-climate-injustice-0

Balibar, Étienne (2018) *Spinoza, the Transindividual*, trans. Mark G. E. Kelly. Edinburgh: Edinburgh University Press.

Bignall, Simone and Daryle Rigney (2019) 'Indigeneity, Posthumanism and Nomad Thought: Transforming Colonial Ecologies'. In Rosi Braidotti and Simone Bignall (eds), *Posthuman Ecologies: Complexity and Process After Deleuze*. London: Rowman & Littlefield International, pp. 159–82.

Boncardo, Robert (2021) 'An Infinite Internal to the Finite: An Interview with Pierre-François Moreau on *Experience and Eternity in Spinoza*'. In Pierre-François Moreau, *Experience and Eternity in Spinoza*, ed. and trans. Robert Boncardo. Edinburgh: University of Edinburgh Press, pp. 569–600.

Bradley, James (2015) *Clade*. Melbourne: Penguin Random House.

Bradley, James (2020a) 'A Landscape Already Lost'. In Cameron Muir, Kirsten Wehner and Jenny Newell (eds), *Living with the Anthropocene: Love, Loss and Hope in the Face of Environmental Crisis*. Sydney: NewSouth Publishing, pp. 218–38.

Bradley, James (2020b) 'The Library at the End of the World'. *Sydney Review of Books*, October.

Braidotti, Rosi (2019) *Posthuman Knowledge*. Chichester: Wiley.

Braidotti, Rosi (2022) *Posthuman Feminism*. Cambridge: Polity Press.
Braidotti, Rosi and Simone Bignall, eds (2019) *Posthuman Ecologies: Complexity and Process After Deleuze*. London: Rowman & Littlefield International.
Burke, Edmund (2015) *A Philosophical Enquiry into the Sublime and the Beautiful* [1757], ed. Paul Guyer. Oxford: Oxford University Press.
Byrd, Jodi A. (2011) *The Transit of Empire: Indigenous Critiques of Colonialism*. Minneapolis: University of Minnesota Press.
Chandler, Jo (2020) 'Weekend in Gondwana'. In Cameron Muir, Kirsten Wehner and Jenny Newell (eds), *Living with the Anthropocene: Love, Loss and Hope in the Face of Environmental Crisis*. Sydney: NewSouth Publishing, pp. 55–74.
Clark, John (1999) 'Comment: Lloyd and Næss on Spinoza as Ecophilosopher'. In Nina Witoszek and Andrew Brennan (eds), *Philosophical Dialogues: Arne Næss and the Progress of Ecophilosophy*. Lanham: Rowman & Littlefield, pp. 102–6.
Curley, Edwin, ed., trans. (1985) *The Collected Works of Spinoza, Volume I*. Princeton: Princeton University Press.
Curley, Edwin, ed., trans. (2016) *The Collected Works of Spinoza, Volume II*. Princeton: Princeton University Press.
Damasio, Antonio (2003) *Looking for Spinoza: Joy, Sorrow and the Feeling Brain*. Orlando: Harcourt.
Deleuze, Gilles (1988) *Spinoza: Practical Philosophy*, trans. Robert Hurley. San Francisco: City Lights Books.
Deleuze, Gilles (1990) *Expressionism in Philosophy: Spinoza*, trans. Martin Joughin. New York. Zone Books.
Derrida, Jacques (2007) 'An Idea of Flaubert: "Plato's Letter"'. In Jacques Derrida, *Psyche: Inventions of the Other, Volume I*, ed. Peggy Kamuf and Elizabeth Rottenberg. Stanford: Stanford University Press, pp. 299–317.
Descartes, René (1984) *Meditations on First Philosophy* [1641]. In John Cottingham, Robert Stoothoff and Dugald Murdoch, trans., *The Philosophical Writings of Descartes, Volume II*. Cambridge: Cambridge University Press, pp. 12–62.
Descartes, René (1985) *The Passions of the Soul* [1649]. In John Cottingham, Robert Stoothoff and Dugald Murdoch, trans.,

The Philosophical Writings of Descartes, Volume I. Cambridge: Cambridge University Press, pp. 325–404.

Dry, Sarah (2019) *Waters of the World*. Chicago: University of Chicago Press.

Field, Sandra Leonie (2020a) 'The Politics of Being Part of Nature'. *Australasian Philosophical Review*, 4.3, pp. 225–35. [Response to Genevieve Lloyd, 'Reconsidering Spinoza's "Rationalism"'.]

Field, Sandra Leonie (2020b) *Potentia: Hobbes and Spinoza on Power and Popular Politics*. Oxford: Oxford University Press.

Flaubert, Gustave (2005) *Bouvard and Pécuchet*, trans. Mark Polizzotti. Normal: Dalkey Archive Press.

Gatens, Moira (2020) 'The Barking Dog and the Mind of God'. *Australasian Philosophical Review*, 4.3, pp. 216–24. [Response to Genevieve Lloyd, 'Reconsidering Spinoza's "Rationalism"'.]

Gatens, Moira and Genevieve Lloyd (1999) *Collective Imaginings: Spinoza, Past and Present*. London: Routledge.

Gatens, Moira, Justin Steinberg, Aurelia Armstrong, Susan James and Martin Saar (2021) 'Spinoza: Thoughts on Hope in Our Political Present'. *Contemporary Political Theory*, 20.1, pp. 200–31.

Ghosh, Amitav (2016) *The Great Derangement: Climate Change and the Unthinkable*. Chicago: University of Chicago Press.

Ghosh, Amitav (2021) *The Nutmeg's Curse: Parables for a Planet in Crisis*. London: John Murray.

Haraway, Donna (2003) *The Companion Species Manifesto: Dogs, People and Significant Otherness*. Chicago: Prickly Paradigm Press.

Head, Lesley (2016) *Hope and Grief in the Anthropocene: Re-conceptualising Human–Nature Relations*. Abingdon: Routledge.

Hübner, Karolina (2020) 'Representation and Mind-Body Identity in Spinoza's Philosophy'. *Journal of the History of Philosophy*, 60.1, pp. 47–77.

James, Susan (2020) *Spinoza on Learning to Live Together* [ebook]. Oxford: Oxford University Press.

James, Susan (2021) 'The Interdependence of Hope and Fear'. In Moira Gatens, Justin Steinberg, Aurelia Armstrong, Susan James and Martin Saar, 'Spinoza: Thoughts on Hope in Our Political Present'. *Contemporary Political Theory*, 20.1, pp. 200–3.

Jaquet, Chantal (2018) *Affects, Actions and Passions in Spinoza: The Unity of Body and Mind*, trans. Tatiana Reznichenko. Edinburgh: Edinburgh University Press.

Jaquet, Chantal (2021) 'Figures du Temps Pluriel'. *Historia Philosophica*,19, pp. 49–58.

Kant, Immanuel (1952) *The Critique of Judgement* [1790], trans. James Creed Meredith. Oxford: Clarendon Press.

Kant, Immanuel (1960) *Observations on the Feeling of the Beautiful and the Sublime* [1764], trans. John T. Goldthwait. Berkeley; Los Angeles: University of California Press.

Kohn, Eduardo (2013) *How Forests Think: Toward an Anthropology Beyond the Human*. Berkeley: University of California Press.

Kohn, Eduardo (2014) 'Further Thoughts on Sylvan Thinking'. *Journal of Ethnographical Theory*, 4.2, pp. 275–88. [Response to HAU Books Symposium on *How Forests Think*.]

Lanchester, John (2019) *The Wall*. London: Faber & Faber.

Latour, Bruno (2005) *Reassembling the Social: An Introduction to Actor-Network-Theory*. Oxford: Oxford University Press.

Leibniz, Gottfried W. (1985) *Theodicy* [1710], trans. E. M. Huggard. La Salle: Open Court.

Liu Cixin (2013) *The Wandering Earth*, trans. Holger Nahm and Ken Liu. Beijing: Beijing Guomi Digital Technology.

Liu Cixin (2015a) *The Three-Body Problem* (Three-Body Trilogy, Book I), trans. Ken Liu. New York: Head of Zeus.

Liu Cixin (2015b) *The Dark Forest* (Three-Body Trilogy, Book II), trans. Joel Martinson. New York: Tor.

Liu Cixin (2016) *Death's End* (Three-Body Trilogy, Book III), trans. Ken Liu. London: Head of Zeus.

Lloyd, G. E. R. (2015) *Analogical Investigations: Historical and Cross-Cultural Perspectives on Human Reasoning*. Cambridge: Cambridge University Press.

Lloyd, G. E. R. (2017) 'Fortunes of Analogy'. *Australasian Philosophical Review*, 1.3, pp. 236–49.

Lloyd, Genevieve (1980) 'Spinoza's Environmental Ethics'. *Inquiry*, 23.3, pp. 293–311. [Reprinted in Nina Witoszek and Andrew Brennan, eds (1999) *Philosophical Dialogues: Arne*

Næss and the Progress of Ecophilosophy. Lanham: Rowman & Littlefield, pp. 73–90.]
Lloyd, Genevieve (1994) *Part of Nature: Self-Knowledge in Spinoza's Ethics*. Ithaca; London: Cornell University Press.
Lloyd, Genevieve (1996) *Routledge Philosophy Guidebook to Spinoza and the Ethics*. Abingdon: Routledge.
Lloyd, Genevieve (2017) 'Spinoza'. In Stephen Leach and James Tartaglia (eds), *Consciousness and the Great Philosophers*. Abingdon; New York: Routledge, pp. 82–8.
Lloyd, Genevieve (2018a) *Reclaiming Wonder: After the Sublime*. Edinburgh: Edinburgh University Press.
Lloyd, Genevieve (2018b) 'Spinoza and the Meaning of Life'. In Stephen Leach and James Tartaglia (eds), *The Meaning of Life and the Great Philosophers*. Abingdon; New York: Routledge, pp. 135–41.
Lloyd, Genevieve (2020a) 'Hope and Optimism: A Spinozist Perspective on COVID-19'. *Journal of Bioethical Inquiry*, 17.4, pp. 503–6.
Lloyd, Genevieve (2020b) 'Reconsidering Spinoza's "Rationalism"'. *Australasian Philosophical Review*, 4.3, pp. 196–215.
Lloyd, Genevieve (2020c) 'Spinoza's Reason Revisited'. *Australasian Philosophical Review*, 4.3, pp. 271–87.
Lloyd, Genevieve (2023) 'Covid and Climate Change: Rethinking Human and Non-human in Western Philosophy'. *Journal of Bioethical Inquiry*. https://doi.org/10.1007/s11673-023-10277-0
Lord, Beth, ed. (2018) *Spinoza's Philosophy of Ratio*. Edinburgh: Edinburgh University Press.
Lord, Beth, ed. (2020) 'We Are Nature'. *Aeon*, 28 April. https://aeon.co/essays/even-the-anthropocene-is-nature-at-work-transforming-itself
Marston, Steph (2020) 'Interrogating Understanding in *Conatus*: A Commentary on Genevieve Lloyd's "Reconsidering Spinoza's 'Rationalism'"'. *Australasian Philosophical Review*, 4.3, pp. 266–70.
Mathews, Freya (2021) *The Ecological Self*, Routledge Classics Edition. Abingdon: Routledge.
Moreau, Pierre-François (2021) *Experience and Eternity in Spinoza*,

ed. and trans. Robert Boncardo. Edinburgh: Edinburgh University Press.

Muir, Cameron, Kirsten Wehner and Jenny Newell, eds (2020) *Living with the Anthropocene: Love, Loss and Hope in the Face of Environmental Crisis*. Sydney: NewSouth Publishing.

Nadler, Steven (2020) *Think Least of Death: Spinoza on How To Live And How To Die*. Princeton; Oxford: Princeton University Press.

Næss, Arne (1973) 'The Shallow and the Deep, Long-Range Ecology Movement: A Summary'. *Inquiry*, 16.1/4, pp. 95–100. [Reprinted in Nina Witoszek and Andrew Brennan, eds (1999) *Philosophical Dialogues: Arne Næss and the Progress of Ecophilosophy*. Lanham: Rowman & Littlefield, pp. 3–7.]

Næss, Arne (1977) 'Spinoza and Ecology'. *Philosophia*, 7.1, pp. 45–54.

Næss, Arne (1980) 'Environmental Ethics and Spinoza's Ethics: Comments on Genevieve Lloyd's Article'. *Inquiry*, 23.3, pp. 313–25. [Reprinted in Nina Witoszek and Andrew Brennan, eds (1999) *Philosophical Dialogues: Arne Naess and the Progress of Ecophilosophy*. Lanham: Rowman & Littlefield, pp. 91–101.]

Næss, Arne (1999) 'Response to Jon Wetlesen'. In Nina Witoszek and Andrew Brennan (eds), *Philosophical Dialogues: Arne Næss and the Progress of Ecophilosophy*. Lanham: Rowman & Littlefield, pp. 418–19.

Neale, Jonathan (2019) 'Social Collapse and Climate Breakdown'. *The Ecologist*, 8 May. https://theecologist.org/2019/may/08/social-collapse-and-climate-breakdown

Newstead, Anne (2020) 'Knowledge Beyond Reason in Spinoza's Epistemology: *Scientia Intuitiva* and *Amor Dei Intellectualis*'. *Australasian Philosophical Review*, 4.3, pp. 250–8. [Response to Genevieve Lloyd, 'Reconsidering Spinoza's "Rationalism"'.]

Noble, Denis (2017) *Dance to the Tune of Life: Biological Relativity*. Cambridge: Cambridge University Press.

Pascal, Blaise (1996) *Pensées*, intro. and trans. A. J. Krailsheimer. Harmondsworth: Penguin.

Peden, Knox (2020) 'Sin and Sensibility: A Response to Genevieve Lloyd's Reconsideration of Spinoza's Rationalism'. *Australasian Philosophical Review*, 4.3, pp. 236–42.

Peirce, Charles S. (1958) 'Questions Concerning Certain Faculties Claimed for Man' [1868]. In Philip P. Wiener (ed.), *Charles S. Peirce: Selected Writings (Values in a Universe of Chance)*. New York: Dover Publications, pp. 15–38.

Porter, Max (2015) *Grief Is the Thing with Feathers*. London: Faber & Faber.

Riley, Denise (2019) *Time Lived, Without Its Flow*, intro. Max Porter. London: Picador.

Robinson, Kim Stanley (1992a) *Green Mars*. London: HarperCollins.

Robinson, Kim Stanley (1992b) *Red Mars*. London: HarperCollins.

Robinson, Kim Stanley (1996) *Blue Mars*. London: HarperCollins.

Robinson, Kim Stanley (2017) *New York 2140*. London: Orbit Books.

Robinson, Kim Stanley (2020a) 'The Coronavirus is Rewriting Our Imagination'. *New Yorker*, 1 May. https://www.newyorker.com/culture/annals-of-inquiry/the-coronavirus-and-our-future

Robinson, Kim Stanley (2020b) *The Ministry for the Future*. London: Orbit Books.

Rose, Deborah Bird (2017) 'Shimmer: When All You Love Is Being Trashed'. In Anna Tsing, Heather Swanson, Elaine Gan and Nils Bubandt (eds), *Arts of Living on a Damaged Planet: Ghosts and Monsters of the Anthropocene*. Minneapolis: University of Minnesota Press, pp. 169–208 [ebook: Ch. 3].

Rose, Deborah Bird (2022) *Shimmer: Flying Fox Exuberance in Worlds of Peril*. Edinburgh: Edinburgh University Press.

Rosenthal, Michael A. (2020) 'A Qualified Defence of Rationalism: On the Role of Analogical Imagination in Spinoza'. *Australasian Philosophical Review*, 4.3, pp. 243–9. [Response to Genevieve Lloyd, 'Reconsidering Spinoza's 'Rationalism'.]

Rovelli, Carlo (2015) *Seven Brief Lessons on Physics*, trans. Simon Carnell and Erica Segre. London: Allen Lane.

Rovelli, Carlo (2018) *The Order of Time*, trans. Erica Segre and Simon Carnell. London: Allen Lane.

Russell, Bertrand (2010) 'The Philosophy of Logical Atomism' [1918]. In David Pears (ed.), *Russell's Logical Atomism*. Abingdon: Routledge, pp. 1–125.

Ryan, John Charles (2020) 'Kelp', in Cameron Muir, Kirsten Wehner and Jenny Newell (eds), *Living with the Anthropocene: Love, Loss and Hope in the Face of Environmental Crisis*. Sydney: NewSouth Publishing, pp. 187–97.

Shah, Sonia (2021) *The Next Great Migration: The Story of Movement on a Changing Planet*, paperback edn. London: Bloomsbury.

Sharp, Hasana (2011) *Spinoza and the Politics of Renaturalization*. Chicago; London: University of Chicago Press.

Steegmuller, Francis and Barbara Bray, eds, trans. (1993) *Flaubert–Sand: The Correspondence of Gustave Flaubert and George Sand*. London: Harvill.

Stengers, Isabelle (2010) *Cosmopolitics I*, trans. Robert Bononno. Minneapolis: University of Minnesota Press.

Tsing, Anna, Heather Swanson, Elaine Gan and Nils Bubandt, eds (2017) *Arts of Living on a Damaged Planet: Ghosts and Monsters of the Anthropocene*. Minneapolis: University of Minnesota Press.

Vardoulakis, Dimitris (2020) *Spinoza, The Epicurean: Authority and Utility in Materialism*. Edinburgh: University of Edinburgh Press.

Veit, Walter (2020) 'Dennett and Spinoza'. *Australasian Philosophical Review*, 4.3, pp. 259–65. [Response to Genevieve Lloyd, 'Reconsidering Spinoza's "Rationalism"'.]

Voltaire (2006) *Candide, or Optimism* [1759], trans. Theo Cuffe. London: Penguin.

Witoszek, Nina and Andrew Brennan, eds (1999) *Philosophical Dialogues: Arne Næss and the Progress of Ecophilosophy*. Lanham: Rowman & Littlefield.

Index

active v. passive emotions, 71–5, 88
adequate ideas, 42, 44, 47–8, 51, 54, 68, 86–7, 88–9, 120, 143
affects, 69–70, 94–5, 126
 and climate change, 169
 interplay of, 180–1
 mind's limited power over, 85–7
 and reason, 116–17, 117–18
 see also emotions; fear; hope; joy; passions; sadness
agency, 4, 5, 113, 145, 151, 161–2
amor, 109
analogical thinking, 148–9
animals, 26, 27, 28–9, 91, 110; see also non-human and human
Anthropocene, 5, 161–2
anthropocentricity, 28, 34
Aotearoa-New Zealand, 151–2
Aristotle, 25, 112
Arts of Living on a Damaged Planet (Tsing et al.), 64
asylum seekers, 162, 163
Australia, 151, 152
Australian bushfires 2019–20, 63

Balibar, É., 166–7
'best possible' world, 61, 62
Bignall, S., 152–3
biological sciences, 169

bodies see human bodies; mind-body dualism
bondage, 85–7, 103
borders, 162–7
Bradley, J., 63, 176
Burke, E., 11–12

Candide (Voltaire), 62
caritas, 109
Cartesian dualism, 31, 150, 155, 156, 169, 182–4
Cartesian model of knowledge, 3–4, 6, 31, 35, 36–7, 38
 Spinoza's critique of, 2–3, 4, 36, 148–9, 149–50
Cartesian model of the mind
 Spinoza's critique of, 69, 116
 see also Cartesian dualism
Cartesian model of thought, 31, 155
 Spinoza's critique of, 164–5
causal relations, 138
certainty, 2, 36–7, 45, 46, 56, 103;
 see also uncertainty
Cixin Liu see Liu Cixin
Clade (Bradley), 176
climate change, 28, 145–6
 and border control, 162–7
 and essence, 114
 The Great Derangement (Ghosh), 155

climate change (cont.)
  and Indigenous knowledge,
    150–1, 153, 154–5
  and science fiction, 174–9
climate change discourse, 1–2, 4–5,
    107–8, 185
  and affects, 169
  limitations of, 174
  'more than human', 29, 32, 33
climate change emotion, 58–61,
    171
climate change grief, 63–6, 82
climate science, 147–8
collaborations, 90–1, 94, 112, 166,
    174
collective grief, 65–6
collective power, 113–14
companion species, 161
compassion, 109
conatus, 40–2, 67, 111, 114, 160,
    165
confidence, 80, 81, 96, 99
Critique of Judgement (Kant), 11, 12
cross-cultural understanding,
    150–5
Curley, E., 78, 109, 124
cypress trees, 32

death, fear of, 126–9, 130, 131–2,
    143
deductive reason, 122–3, 149
'deep' ecology, 24, 25–6
Deleuze, G., 139, 169–72, 179
Derrida, J., 172–3
Descartes, R., 91, 111–12; see also
    Cartesian dualism; Cartesian
    model of knowledge; Cartesian
    model of the mind; Cartesian
    model of thought
desire *see* human desire
despair, 61, 65, 80–1, 98, 99
Dickinson, E., 64
doubt, 80–1, 96, 99, 100, 103
Dry, S., 147–8

ecological attitudes, 24–5, 27, 34,
    161
Elements of the Laws (Hobbes), 113
embodiment, 32, 71, 120–2, 121–3,
    123–6
  within Nature, 95, 97
emotions
  active v. passive, 71–5, 88
  interaction with reason and
    imagination, 67–71, 77, 174
  interplay of, 180–1
  see also affects; climate change
    emotion; climate change
    grief; fear; hope; joy; 'loving-
    kindness'; passions; sadness;
    'structure of feeling'; wonder
empathy, 66, 110
emulation, 110–11
'Enlightenment thought', 180
Environmental Philosophy, 24–6
equality, 140
error, 37, 38, 39, 55–6, 67
  and imagination, 52–4
essences, 114, 123–4, 127, 143, 165,
    166–7
eternity, 121–3, 130
ethics, Māori, 152
Ethics (Spinoza), 2–3
  rationalism, 7–8
  structure, 9
  trajectory, 56–7
Experience and Eternity (Moreau),
    185–6
expression, 138, 139
Expressionism in Philosophy
    (Deleuze), 139
extension, 15, 16, 17, 34, 138; *see
    also* things and thought

fear, 78–83, 96–101
  of death, 126–9, 130, 131–2, 143
  and futurity, 107–8
  politics of, 101–6
Fixer, The (Malamud), 170

Flaubert, G., 172–3
free will, 4, 36, 37, 38, 114
freedom, 40–2, 53, 54–6, 107, 144–6, 168
'Freedom and Nature' (James), 145, 146
friendship, 90, 92, 109, 111, 112; see also 'loving-kindness'
futurity, 59–60, 64–5, 80, 81, 98–9, 107–8
and science fiction, 174–9

générosité, 111–12
Ghosh, A., 155–6, 162, 175
God, 14–18, 23, 34, 85, 93, 103, 138
and essences, 123–4
and knowledge, 119–20, 120–1
love of, 121, 126, 127, 128–9, 129–32
and reason, 42–4, 49–52
goodness see human goodness
Great Derangement, The (Ghosh), 155, 175
grief see climate change grief
Grief Is the Thing with Feathers (Porter), 64

Haraway, D., 161
Head, L., 28–9, 60, 150–1
Hegel, G.W.F., 14
Hobbes, T., 113, 114, 166
hope, 60–1, 78–83, 96–101
and futurity, 107–8
and grief, 64, 65
politics of, 101–6
v. optimism, 61–2, 65
How Forests Think (Kohn), 156–7
human agency see agency
human and non-human, 4–5, 13, 23–4, 28–30, 32–5, 85
Indigenous knowledge, 151–2
post-colonial imagining, 155–60
post-humanism, 160–2

see also animals; humanity's place in Nature
human bodies, 17, 34, 44, 103, 138–42; see also mind-body dualism
human bondage, 85–7, 103
human desire, 74, 78, 86, 114
human error, 37, 38, 39, 55–6, 67
and imagination, 52–4
human exceptionalism, 24
human goodness, 85–7, 89, 91–2
human knowing see knowledge
human minds, 139
and affects, 85–7
and bodies, 17, 34, 53, 138–42
embodiment, 32, 71, 121–3, 123–6
and freedom, 55, 88, 168
and futurity, 98–9
and God, 43, 48–52, 88, 120–1, 129–32
and human freedom, 40–2
and ideas, 42–4, 45–8, 54–6
and Nature, 158–60, 180–1
in Pascal, 22
and wonder, 75–7
see also imagination; knowledge; mind-body dualism; reason
human supremacy, 3–4, 14, 28–9, 58, 90, 144; see also human and non-human
human well-being, 90, 91–2
humanity's place in Nature, 1–2, 25, 58, 89, 103; see also human and non-human; human minds: and Nature

'Idea of Flaubert, An' (Derrida), 172
ideas, 40, 45–8, 54–6
adequate, 51, 120, 143: v. inadequate, 42–4, 47–8, 68, 86–7, 88–9
'ideas of ideas', 45, 46, 55

imagination, 38–40, 44, 49, 137, 150
  and affects, 86, 98, 108
  and doubt, 100
  and error, 52–4
  interaction with reason and emotion, 67–71, 77, 174
  and reason, 39, 99, 119, 122–3
  Western, 155
  and wonder, 76
  see also postcolonial imagining
imitation, 110–11
immensity, feeling of, 20–2
inadequate ideas, 42, 43–4, 48, 54, 68, 86, 88–9
Indigenous knowledge, 150–5
ingenium, 180–1

James, S., 145, 146
Jaquet, C., 108, 139–40, 180
jealousy, 72–3
joy, 81, 106, 112, 120, 126–9
  and hope, 82–3, 97, 108
  and reason, 87, 94, 117
  'structure of feeling' as, 177
  and wonder, 95

Kant, I., 11, 12–13, 136
knowledge, 17–18, 33–5, 71
  Cartesian model of, 3–4, 6, 31, 35, 36–7, 38: Spinoza's critique of, 2–3, 4, 36, 148–9, 149–50
  and the Good Life, 35–8
  and imagination, 39–40, 44
  Indigenous, 150–5
  intuitive, 118–20, 137, 142–3: and God, 120–1, 125, 131; and joy, 126–8
  see also human minds; imagination; rationalism; reason
knowledge systems, alternative, 148–9; see also Indigenous knowledge
Kohn, E., 156–7

Lanchester, J., 163, 174
language, philosophy of, 156
Latour, B., 161
Leibniz, G.W., 61, 62, 138–9
literature see science fiction
Liu Cixin, 175–6
Lloyd, G.E.R., 148–9, 154
Longinus, 11, 12
love of God, 121, 126, 127, 128–9, 129–32
'loving-kindness', 109–12, 115, 162, 167

Malamud, B., 170
Māori ethics, 152
Mars Trilogy (Robinson), 178–9
Mathews, F., 160
matter see extension; things and thought
mauri, 152
metaphysical optimism, 61–2
migration, 164, 165–6; see also refugees
mind-body dualism, 31, 150, 155, 156, 169, 182–4
Ministry of the Future, The (Robinson), 177–8, 181
'more than human', 29, 32, 33
Moreau, P.-F., 185–6
mortality, 59, 121–3, 130, 131–2

Nadler, S., 142–3
Næss, A., 24–5, 27, 34, 161
Nature, 21–2, 85
  and freedom, 144–6
  and God, 15
  human embodiment within, 95, 97
  and human minds, 158–60, 180–1
  humanity's place in, 1–2, 29–30, 58, 89, 103
  and reason, 19–20, 23–4, 89–93, 134–6, 143–4
  in Romanticism, 10–13, 14

wholeness of, 147, 167
see also animals; non-human and human
Neale, J., 166
necessity, 136–7, 144, 145
New York 2140 (Robinson), 178
New Zealand *see* Aotearoa-New Zealand
Next Great Migration, The (Shah), 164
nobility, 72
Noble, D., 169
non-human and human, 4–5, 13, 23–4, 28–30, 32–5, 85, 90–1
  Indigenous knowledge, 151–2
  post-colonial imagining, 155–60
  post-humanism, 160–2
  see also animals; Nature: humanity's place in
Novalis, 14
novels *see* science fiction
Nutmeg's Curse, The (Ghosh), 155, 162

octopuses, 28–9
Oldenberg, H., 158
On the Sublime (Longinus), 11
optimism, 60, 61–2, 65
Order of Time, The (Rovelli), 168

parallelism, 138–42
Pascal, B., 20–2
passions, 68, 71, 86, 92, 116–17, 141
  and reason, 87–9, 93–6, 105, 107, 117–18
  see also affects; emotions; fear; hope; joy; sadness
passive emotions *see* active v. passive emotions; passions
Peirce, C.S., 156
people-smuggling, 163
philosophy of language, 156
'Poem on the Lisbon Disaster' (Voltaire), 61

Political Treatise (Spinoza), 103–6
politics of hope and fear, 101–6
Porter, M., 64
post-humanism, 160–2
postcolonial imagining, 155–60
power, 113–15

rationalism, 7–8, 143; *see also* knowledge; reason
reality and thought, 148–50
reason, 149–50
  deductive, 122–3, 149
  and emotions / affects, 67–71, 77, 174: active v. passive emotions, 71–5, 88 (*see also* reason: and passions)
  and freedom, 54–6
  and God, 42–4, 49–52
  and hope and fear, 96–7
  and imagination, 39, 77, 99, 119, 122–3, 174
  and intuitive knowledge, 119, 131, 142–3
  and joy, 87, 94, 117
  limitations of, 17
  and Nature, 19–20, 21–2, 23–4, 89–93, 134–6, 143–4
  and necessity, 136–7
  and passions, 87–9, 93–6, 99, 105, 107, 116–18
  and the sublime, 11–13
  supremacy of, 3–4, 14
  and time, 82
  see also human minds; knowledge; rationalism
refugees, 162–3, 166; *see also* migration
respect, 110
Rigney, D., 152–3
Riley, D., 64–6
Robinson, K.S., 176–9
Romanticism, 3, 20, 172
  Nature in, 10–13, 14
  and Spinoza, 13–15

Rose, D.B., 153
Rovelli, C., 168
Russell, B., 17–18

sadness, 59, 81, 82, 96, 108, 126
Sand, G., 172
scepticism, 35
science fiction, 174–9
Seneca, 65, 78–9
Seven Brief Lessons on Physics (Rovelli), 168
Shah, S., 164
'shallow' ecology, 24–5
Sharp, H., 26–7
'speaking as country', 152
speciesism, 91
Spinoza and the Politics of Renaturalization (Sharp), 26–7
Spinoza, B.
  appeal of work, 169–74, 179
  and climate change discourse, 185
  and Environmental Philosophy, 24–6
  family, 184
  and rationalism, 7–8
  reading and interpreting, 5–7
  and Romanticism, 13–15
Spinoza: Practical Philosophy (Deleuze), 169–72
Stoicism, 65, 78–9, 83, 127, 141, 142–4
'structure of feeling', 177, 180

sublime, the, 11–13
submarine kelp zones, 32–3
sympathy, 66, 94, 109

temporality / time, 64–6, 80, 82
tenacity, 72
Theodicy (Leibniz), 61
Theological-Political Treatise (Spinoza), 101–2, 134–5, 172
things and thought, 137–42
Think Least of Death (Nadler), 142–3
thought, 15, 16, 17, 34, 92, 136
  Cartesian model of, 31, 155;
  Spinoza's critique of, 164–5
  and reality, 148–50
  and things, 137–42
  see also 'Enlightenment thought'
Three-Body Problem, The (Liu), 175–6
Time Lived, Without Its Flow (Riley), 64–6
truth, 35, 37, 38, 43, 44, 45, 47

uncertainty, 59, 60, 81–2, 96, 98; *see also* certainty

Voltaire, 61–2, 80, 98

Wall, The (Lanchester), 163, 174–5
Waters of the World (Dry), 147–8
well-being, 90, 91–2
Williams, R., 177
wonder, 75–8, 95–6